Sets & Sashings

FOR QUILTS

PHYLLIS D. MILLER

American Quilter's Society

P. O. Box 3290 • Paducah, KY 42002-3290

Located in Paducah, Kentucky, the American Quilter's Society (AQS) is dedicated to promoting the accomplishments of today's quilters. Through its publications and events, AQS strives to honor today's quiltmakers and their work and to inspire future creativity and innovation in quiltmaking.

EDITOR: BONNIE K. BROWNING

BOOK DESIGN: TOM SULLIVAN

ILLUSTRATIONS: TOM SULLIVAN, JARRETT SIMS, AND ELAINE WILSON

COVER DESIGN: MICHAEL BUCKINGHAM

PHOTOGRAPHY: CHARLES R. LYNCH

Library of Congress Cataloging-in-Publication Data
Miller, Phyllis D.
     Sets and sashings for quilts / Phyllis D. Miller
        p. cm.
     Includes bibliographical references and index.
     ISBN 1-57432-740-2
     1. Patchwork--Patterns. 2. Quilting--Patterns. I. Title.
TT835 .M538 2000
746.46'041--dc21
                                  00-009593

Additional copies of this book may be ordered from the American Quilter's Society, PO Box 3290, Paducah, KY 42002-3290

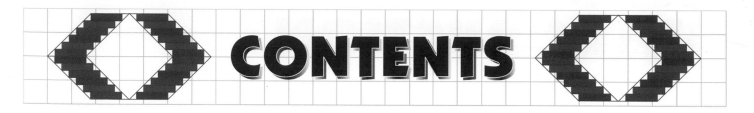

CONTENTS

INTRODUCTION

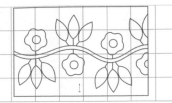

Have you said or do you know someone who has said, "What would you do with these blocks?" or "How do I put these blocks together in a quilt?"

For many years, I have taught a Sets and Sashings class where the participants in the class could bring a set of their blocks for help in deciding how to put them together. Many of the sets of blocks had been made in beginning quilting classes and were sampler blocks used to learn a variety of skills. What to do with them was a mystery! In this book, I hope you will find answers and discover that any set or any sashing is easier to do than it appears.

The General Instructions section of the book includes bed sizes, how to draft many of the plain blocks needed in constructing a quilt top, how to make a **paper quilt**, and other tidbits on using this book.

In the Sets section of the book, you will find all of the set options from simple straight block-to-block construction to medallion and random sets. Each different set style is described in detail with instructions for pattern drafting where needed, and how to sew the sets together.

In the Sashings section of the book, I have included many varieties of sashings that can be used with plain, pieced, or appliquéd blocks. Many of the sashings are so interesting that they can be used with plain blocks to make a quilt top. Each sashing has instructions for sizing, cutting, and sewing. Many sashings have patterns included. There is a paper quilt worksheet for each different sashing for you to use in choosing a sashing and designing your quilt top.

When writing the instructions, I tried to give you the easiest construction method. There are many ways to reach the same end. Improve upon my instructions when you can. I hope this book will give you many inspirations and the information will prove helpful when you create quilts that are uniquely yours.

■ Look for this block throughout the text. It refers you to the hint at the bottom of the page.

✿ Look for this flower throughout the text. This information makes drafting and construction easier.

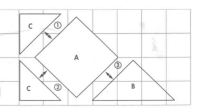

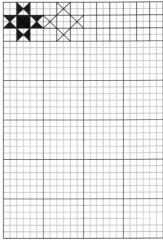

The words "drafting" and "designing" scare many quilters. When these words are used, **do not fear**. Quilters have been drafting and designing for centuries, and if they could do it, so can you and I. Look at both as processes that make quiltmaking fun.

Let's start with designing. It is helpful to have a game plan, so here are directions for making a **paper quilt**. Making a paper quilt for a guide is much easier than laying quilt blocks out on the floor or a bed and then moving the blocks around until they are pleasing. It is also more fun. Nothing is more frustrating than moving blocks several times and not being able to remember how they looked in previous moves.

MAKING A PAPER QUILT

To make your own paper quilt, you will need ¼" grid graph paper, a lead pencil, a ruler with at least ⅛" marks, and paper-cutting scissors. Color pencils are also handy but not necessary.

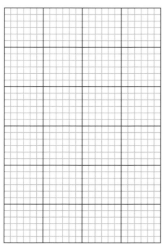

Decide how many inches one square on the graph paper will represent. For example, for a nine-patch block such as the Ohio Star, each square could represent 1½". Each paper block will need six ¼" graph paper squares or a 1½" measured square. Draw squares this size on the graph paper (Fig. G-1).

Fig. G–1

Next, fill the squares with blocks you have or want to make. The Ohio Star block has been used in the example shown in Figure G-2. Shade in or color the design in the blocks or use them as is. ◼

Using paper scissors, cut out the paper blocks. When the blocks have been placed on the graph paper in an arrangement that you like, use a restickable adhesive glue stick to hold the little paper blocks in place (Photo 1).

Fig. G–2

Photo 1. Photo by author.

USING A DESIGN WORKSHEET

Design worksheets have been provided for each Set (pages 26 – 33) and Sashing style (pages 92 – 125). These pre-drawn worksheets can be photocopied to make it easy for you to begin your quilt. By inserting your paper blocks in the squares, you can see how the setting or sashing looks. If the worksheets show black and white blocks as a guide, place your blocks over the printed ones.

◼ **Hint:** *For the worksheets, each quilt block should be drawn in a 1" square. Each 1" square would represent the finished size of the block. For designing purposes, the paper block does not have to be accurate. Blocks can be copied from pattern identification books and used in the paper quilt. You can also use squares of plain or construction paper to represent the quilt block.*

Most of the sashings from the Sashings section of the book are shown in a straight set. If this is the set that you have chosen, simply place your paper blocks in the block squares, using the Straight Set worksheet. ▪

Photo 2.

If you would like to change the set from the one used in the worksheet quilt, use scissors to cut apart the photocopies of the worksheet quilt. First, cut the paper quilt to obtain rows (Photo 2).

Next, rearrange the rows to make a new set. Use a pencil and ruler to divide the little paper blocks into triangles or other shapes, if needed. In Photo 3, the rows have been rearranged for a Diagonal Set.

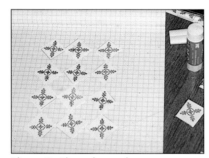

Photo 3. Photo by author.

The size of the worksheet paper quilt can be changed by taking off or adding blocks or rows to make the quilt smaller or larger.

Many of the sashing designs in the worksheet quilts have been shaded light and dark so the design is more prominent. To see how the sashings would look with the light/dark changed or how they would look in color, place tracing paper over the paper quilt and do a new shading or coloring (Photo 4).

Photo 4. Photo by author.

DETERMINING THE SIZE

Part of designing a quilt top is finding out what size it will be or getting it to be the desired size. Several things combine to determine what size the top will be when sewn together. The size of the blocks, the set, and the width of the sashing play parts in the final width and length of the quilt. The information given for determining the size of the quilt is just for the blocks and sashings. If borders are used, those figures are added to determine the finished size of the quilt top.

When determining the size of the quilt, measuring the block is important. Here are some tips for measuring a block. The finished size (less seam allowances) is always used. The arrows in the block shapes indicate how to measure (Fig. G-3).

When you do not have a block to physically measure, it is helpful to know the diagonal measurements of square blocks. You can figure the diagonal by multiplying the width of the block by 1.414. For quick reference, use the chart for measurements of standard blocks.

QUICK REFERENCE FOR DIAGONAL BLOCK MEASUREMENTS			
Finished Block Size	**Diagonal Measure**	**Finished Block Size**	**Diagonal Measure**
2" block =	2 ⅞"	10" block =	14 ⅛"
3" block =	4 ¼"	12" block =	17"
4" block =	5 ⅝"	14" block =	19 ⅞"
5" block =	7 ⅛"	16" block =	22 ⅝"
6" block =	8 ½"	18" block =	25 ½"
7" block =	9 ⅞"	20" block =	28 ¼"
8" block =	11 ¼"	24" block =	34"
9" block =	12 ¾"		

The blocks and sashings of a quilt are often designed to cover only the top of the bed. If possible, measure the actual bed for which the quilt is being designed. The standard size measurements for most mattresses are shown in the Standard Mattress Sizes chart.

▪ ***Hint:*** *Make a photocopy of the worksheet page so the paper blocks can be glued down. This makes it easier to use the design worksheet when constructing the quilt top. For sets other than the straight set, make two or three copies of the worksheet to cut up.*

STANDARD MATTRESS SIZES	
Crib – 23" x 46"	Double – 54" x 75"
Youth – 32" x 66"	Queen – 60" x 80"
Twin – 39" x 75"	King – 78" x 80"
X-long Twin – 39" x 80"	

For wall quilts, plan the quilt to fit the wall where the quilt will hang. For quilts designed specifically for entry in a contest, be sure to read the rules and plan your quilt with the minimum and maximum sizes in mind.

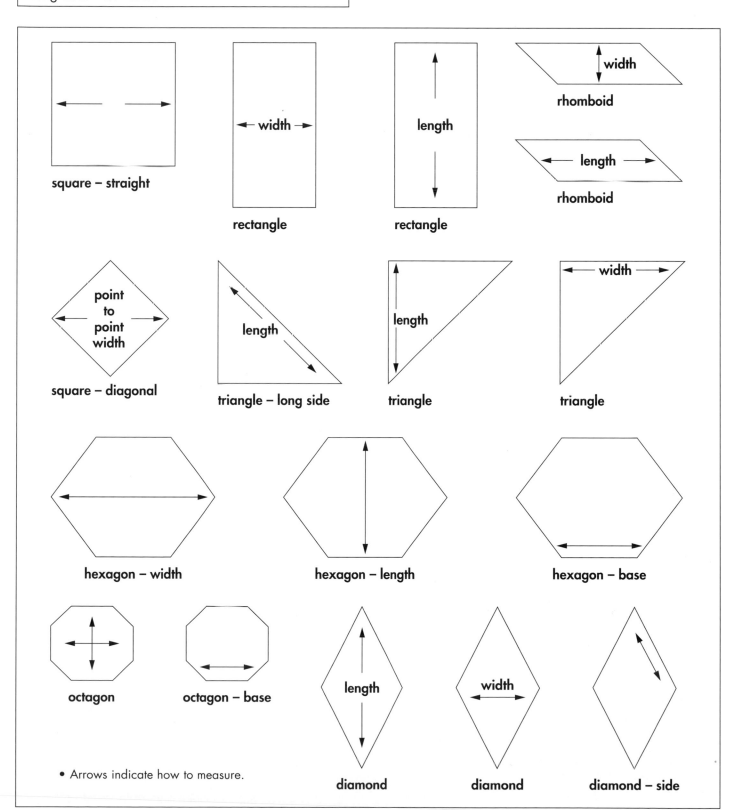

Fig. G – 3 Block Shapes

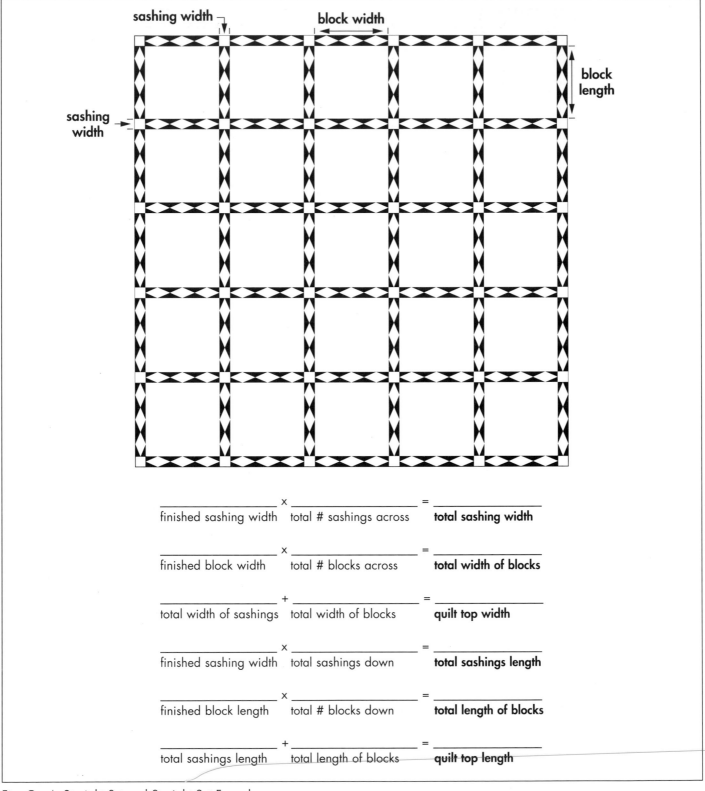

Fig. G – 4 Straight Set and Straight Set Formula

Use the formulas for Straight Set (Fig. G-4) and Diagonal Set (Fig. G-5) as guides to figure the size of your quilt.

For any of the other sets, use the same measuring methods to determine the width and length of the quilt top. In addition to these measurements, remember to add border widths and/or lengths, if used, to come up with the final quilt top size.

Sets & Sashings for Quilts – Phyllis D. Miller

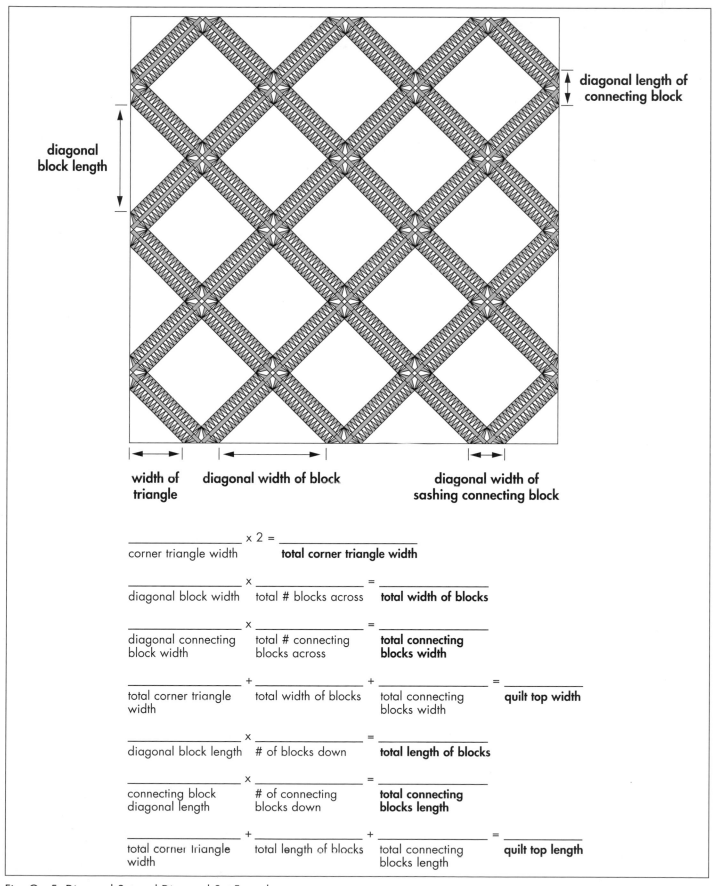

diagonal length of connecting block

diagonal block length

width of triangle

diagonal width of block

diagonal width of sashing connecting block

_____ x 2 = _____
corner triangle width   **total corner triangle width**

_____ x _____ = _____
diagonal block width   total # blocks across   **total width of blocks**

_____ x _____ = _____
diagonal connecting   total # connecting   **total connecting**
block width   blocks across   **blocks width**

_____ + _____ + _____ = _____
total corner triangle   total width of blocks   total connecting   **quilt top width**
width   blocks width

_____ x _____ = _____
diagonal block length   # of blocks down   **total length of blocks**

_____ x _____ = _____
connecting block   # of connecting   **total connecting**
diagonal length   blocks down   **blocks length**

_____ + _____ + _____ = _____
total corner triangle   total length of blocks total connecting   **quilt top length**
width   blocks length

Fig. G – 5 Diagonal Set and Diagonal Set Formula

STRAIGHT SET

In a straight set the blocks of the quilt are sewn together in straight rows that go horizontally across the quilt.

Photo 5. THE FREQUENT FLYER
by Jennifer A. Patriarche. Straight set.
Photo by maker.

Worksheet: Straight Set, page 26.

Size of Quilt Top:

$$\frac{}{\text{finished block width}} \times \frac{}{\text{\# blocks across}} = \frac{}{\textbf{quilt top width}}$$

$$\frac{}{\text{finished block width}} \times \frac{}{\text{\# blocks down}} = \frac{}{\textbf{quilt top length}}$$

Pattern Drafting: None

Sewing: A row or set of blocks will be sewn together in the sequence shown in Figure 1–1.

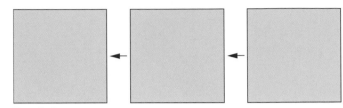

Fig. 1–1

With the right sides of two blocks together, sew block #2 to block #1 to form a unit. See Figure 1–2.

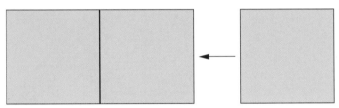

Fig. 1–2

Continue sewing blocks together to make a row or strip the desired width (Fig. 1–3). Make as many rows as you need.

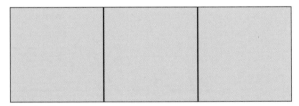

Fig. 1–3

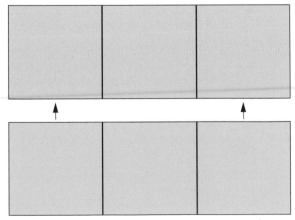

Fig. 1–4

Now, place two rows, right sides together. Pin the two rows together to match the seams of the blocks. Sew the two rows together (Fig. 1–4). Continue sewing the rows together to complete the quilt top.

DIAGONAL SET

In a diagonal set, the blocks are positioned with the corners of the blocks lined up vertically and horizontally on the quilt top. A diagonal set is also called an on-point set; the rows are assembled diagonally across the quilt top.

Worksheet: Diagonal Set, page 27.

Size of the Quilt Top: For the measurement diagonally across a block, see the chart on page 9 or use the formula.

$$\underline{\hspace{3cm}} \times 1.414 = \underline{\hspace{3cm}}$$
finished block size   **diagonal block measure**

$$\underline{\hspace{3cm}} \times \underline{\hspace{2cm}} = \underline{\hspace{2cm}}$$
diagonal block measure   # blocks across   **quilt top width**

$$\underline{\hspace{3cm}} \times \underline{\hspace{2cm}} = \underline{\hspace{2cm}}$$
diagonal block measure   # blocks down   **quilt top length**

Pattern Drafting: Large half-square triangles are needed along the quilt edges and a quarter-square triangle is used in each of the corners. ▪

To find the **size to cut the pattern** for the large half-square triangles that are needed at the ends of the diagonal rows:

$$\underline{\hspace{3cm}} + \tfrac{7}{8}" = \underline{\hspace{3cm}}$$
block finished size   **square size to draft**

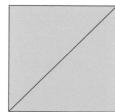

Draw a line on your drafted square diagonally from a lower corner to the opposite upper corner to form two triangles. These triangles now have the seam allowance added and can be used for a pattern to cut the fill-in or large half-square triangles (Fig. 2–1).

Fig. 2–1

Photo 6. SOMETHING WICKED THIS WAY COMES by Carolyn Lynch. Diagonal set. Photo by maker.

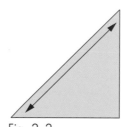

The half-square triangles must be cut with the diagonal or long side of the triangle on the straight grain of the fabric to avoid stretching the edges of the quilt top (Fig. 2–2).

Fig. 2–2

To find the **size to cut the pattern** for the small or corner triangles needed at the four corners of the quilt top:

$$\underline{\hspace{3cm}} + 1\tfrac{1}{4}" = \underline{\hspace{3cm}}$$
block finished size   **square size to draft**

▪ **Hint:** *Draft the pattern on freezer paper and then use the freezer paper draft for the pattern by ironing it onto the right side of the fabric and cutting with a rotary cutter. Four layers can be cut at one time. A freezer paper pattern can be ironed onto fabric three or four times before it loses its adhering capability.*

Fig. 2–3

Draw the square on freezer paper. Mark lines diagonally from upper corners to lower corners to make a drafted pattern like the one in Figure 2–3. The pattern now has the seam allowances added and is ready to iron to the right side of the fabric and cut with a rotary cutter or scissors.

The corner triangles must be cut with the right angle on the straight grain of the fabric (Fig. 2–4).

Fig. 2–4

Sewing: A row will be sewn together starting with a half-square triangle placed with a block, right sides together. Continue sewing another block to the already sewn unit until a whole row that goes diagonally across the quilt top is sewn. See Figure 2–5.

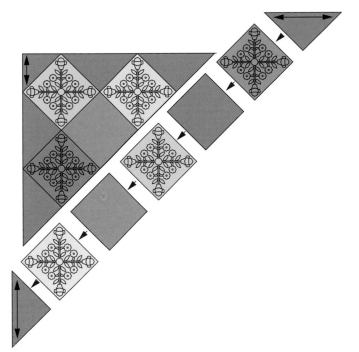
Fig. 2–5

The quilt top is constructed by pinning and sewing the rows together. Be sure to match up the seams of the blocks before sewing. ▪

Be sure that the long side of the half-square triangle is positioned properly at the end of

▪ **Hint:** *It is usually easier to sew the longer units together first.*

each row so the outside edges of the quilt top with be on the straight grain of the fabric. If, for design reasons, the long sides of the triangles are cut on the bias, stay stitch the long side of each triangle before assembling the rows.

HEXAGONAL SET

In a hexagonal set, the block is either a hexagon or a set of blocks that make a hexagon when pieced together. Sewing a hexagonal set will require either pieced or solid half–hexagon blocks units.

Photo 7. SOCCER STARS by Judi Robb. Hexagonal set.

Worksheet: Hexagonal Set, page 28.

Size of Quilt Top: Measure a hexagon or hexagon unit from point to point (Fig. 3–a), from side to side (Fig. 3-b), and the base (Fig. 3–c). Measure the number of units as well (Fig. 3–d).

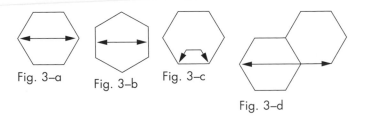
Fig. 3–a   Fig. 3–b   Fig. 3–c   Fig. 3–d

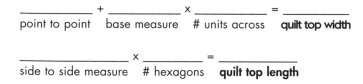

_____ + _____ x _____ = _____
point to point   base measure   # units across   **quilt top width**

_____ x _____ = _____
side to side measure   # hexagons   **quilt top length**

Pattern Drafting: Half of a 60° diamond is needed to fill in the sides of the top to get a straight edge. To draw a diamond in the size needed, use the measurement of the hexagon from side to side. This is the length the diamond needs to be. On a sheet of paper, draw a line vertically down the middle. Use the ruler to make another line across the middle. See Figure 3–1.

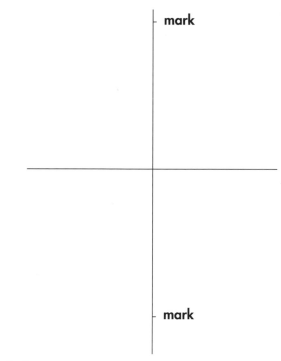

Fig. 3–2

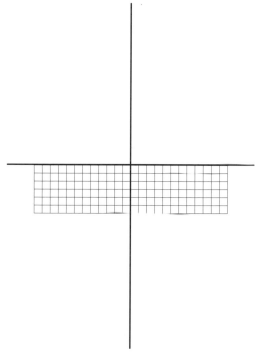

Fig. 3–1

Divide the determined length of the diamond by 2. Place the ruler on the vertical line and make a mark this length above and below the center line as shown in Figure 3–2.

The ruler must have a 30° (half of the 60° diamond point needed) line mark. Place the 30° line of the ruler on the lower part of the vertical line with the end of the 30° line touching the length mark of that line (Fig. 3–3). Mark a line along the ruler edge extending past the center line.

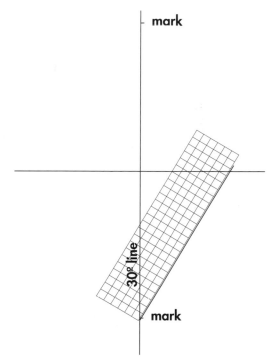

Fig. 3–3

Repeat the steps for the top half of the diamond (Fig. 3–4, page 14). These two new lines will intersect at the middle line of the diamond.

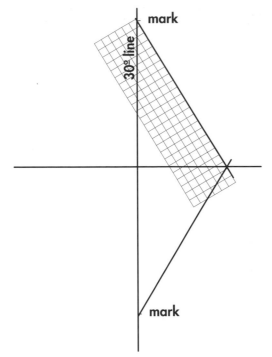

Fig. 3–4

🌼 The lines just marked should cross each other exactly on the center line. If they do not cross exactly, the half diamond has not been drafted correctly. Check the line–up of the ruler and the marks of the lines and fix it now.

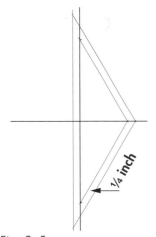

Fig. 3–5

Make a template by adding ¼" seam allowances as shown in Figure 3–5.

A quarter diamond will be needed for two corners and this template can be made by using half of the drafted half diamond and adding seam allowances.

Sewing: The hexagon set requires setting in hexagon units; each side of the hexagons must be sewn separately to join the units together. This set is probably best done by hand sewing but can be machine sewn by being careful to mark and sew only to the points where the seam allowances meet. Do not sew into the seam allowances.

To make a unit as shown in Figure 3–6, place two hexagons right sides together and sew along one side to the corners, starting and stopping ¼" from the edges.

Figure 3–7 shows how a third hexagon will be set in by sewing it to the adjacent open sides of the two–hexagon unit. ◾

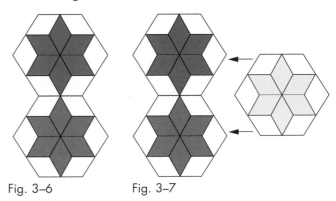

Fig. 3–6   Fig. 3–7

BARS SET
The Bars set is often associated with Amish quilts where the quilt top consists only of bars or vertical strips of fabric. Strippies is another name that is used in the British Isles for the Bars set. Blocks can also be set together in bars or strips. The bars of blocks are separated by strips of fabric. Solid, print, or striped fabric can be used for the sashing or dividing bars.

Worksheet: Bars Set, page 29.

Size of Quilt Top:

_____	÷	_____	=	_____
bed width		finished block width		**# possible bars**

To determine size of sashing strip, decide how many bars can be made from the blocks already made or that will be made.

◾ **Hint:** *The hexagon block units can be sewn together in rows and then join the rows, although it is probably easier to add one block at a time to the already sewn blocks.*

Photo 8. SANDY PINES SEASONAL HOMES
by Ardie Sveadus. Bars set.

$$\frac{\rule{2cm}{0.4pt}}{\text{\# bars}} \times \frac{\rule{4cm}{0.4pt}}{\text{finished block width}} = \frac{\rule{4cm}{0.4pt}}{\textbf{total width of all bars}}$$

$$\frac{\rule{2cm}{0.4pt}}{\substack{\text{bed width}}} \div \frac{\rule{2cm}{0.4pt}}{\substack{\text{total width} \\ \text{of all bars}}} = \frac{\rule{2cm}{0.4pt}}{\substack{\text{inches left} \\ \text{for bars}}} \div \frac{\rule{1cm}{0.4pt}}{\substack{\text{equally}}} = \frac{\rule{1cm}{0.4pt}}{\substack{\textbf{sashing} \\ \textbf{width}}}$$

$$\frac{\rule{3cm}{0.4pt}}{\substack{\text{finished block length}}} \times \frac{\rule{2cm}{0.4pt}}{\substack{\text{\# blocks}}} = \frac{\rule{2cm}{0.4pt}}{\substack{\textbf{sashing strip length}}}$$

Pattern Drafting: None ■

Sewing: Sew the blocks together in bars of the desired length (Fig. 4–1). Place the right sides of the strip of blocks and the sashing strip together and sew. Continue by adding another strip or bar of blocks, sashing strip, blocks, etc. until the quilt top is complete.

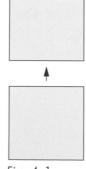

Fig. 4–1

STREAK OF LIGHTNING SET

The Streak of Lightning set, also called Zig–zag, is also sewn in a Bars set. Because it looks more complicated, it is presented as a separate set. Simple pieced blocks can be more exciting in the Streak of Lightning set.

Photo 9. A FEW OF HER FAVORITE THINGS
by Joan Rozek. Streak of Lightning set.
Photo by maker.

Worksheet: Streak of Lightning Set, page 30.

Size of Quilt Top:

$$\frac{\rule{3cm}{0.4pt}}{\substack{\text{bed width}}} \div \frac{\rule{3cm}{0.4pt}}{\substack{\text{finished block} \\ \text{diagonal width}}} = \frac{\rule{3cm}{0.4pt}}{\substack{\textbf{\# possible bars}}}$$

$$\frac{\rule{3cm}{0.4pt}}{\substack{\text{finished block} \\ \text{diagonal width}}} = \frac{\rule{3cm}{0.4pt}}{\substack{\textbf{bar width}}}$$

$$\frac{\rule{3cm}{0.4pt}}{\substack{\text{finished block} \\ \text{diagonal length}}} \times \frac{\rule{2cm}{0.4pt}}{\substack{\text{\# blocks}}} = \frac{\rule{3cm}{0.4pt}}{\substack{\textbf{length of bars}}}$$

■ **Hint:** *The blocks can be on-point in the bars. See page 16 for instructions to draft the triangles with a straight of grain edge needed to make the bar or strip with on-point blocks.*

Fig. 5–1

Fig. 5–2

Pattern Drafting: This set is pieced in strips or bars (Fig. 5–1) and, if pieced blocks are used, half of a pieced block will be needed at the ends of the strips or bars to achieve the lightning or zig-zag. Make templates for the pieces of the block marked with dots in Figure 5–2.

 An assembled pieced block cannot be cut in half and used because seam allowances must be added to the pattern pieces that are along the diagonal of the half-block. These pieces should be cut so the edges on the diagonal of the half-block are cut on the straight grain of the fabric.

To find the **size to cut the pattern** for the half-square side triangles needed to set the on-point blocks into a straight strip or bar:

$$\underline{\hspace{5cm}} + \tfrac{7}{8}" = \underline{\hspace{4cm}}$$
finished size of the block | **size of square to draft**

Fig. 5–3

Draw a line diagonally from a lower corner to the opposite upper corner on your drafted square to form two triangles (Fig. 5–3). These triangles now have the seam allowance added and can be used for the pattern to cut half-square triangles. ◼

The side triangles must be cut with the long side of the triangle on the straight grain of the fabric to avoid stretching the sides of the strips or bars (Fig. 5–4).

To find the **size to cut the pattern** for the small triangles needed at one end of each bar:

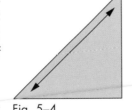

Fig. 5–4

$$\underline{\hspace{5cm}} + 1\tfrac{1}{4}" = \underline{\hspace{4cm}}$$
finished size of the block | **size of square to draft**

Draw the square on freezer paper. Mark lines diagonally from upper corners to lower corners to make a drafted pattern like the one in Figure 5–5. The pattern now has the seam allowances added and is ready to iron to the right side of the fabric and cut with a rotary cutter or scissors. The freezer paper patterns can be ironed to fabric three or four times before they lose their adhering capability.

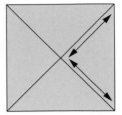

Fig. 5–5

 The small triangles must be cut with the right angle on the straight of grain of the fabric.

Sewing: To make each bar or strip, sew triangles and blocks together in diagonal units (Fig. 5–6). The diagonal units can now be sewn into bars as shown in Figure 5–7.

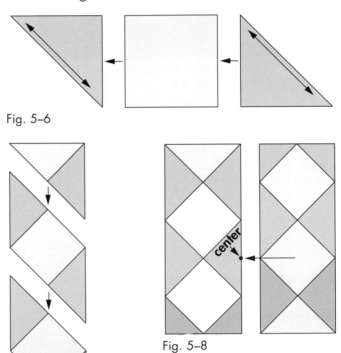

Fig. 5–6

Fig. 5–7

Fig. 5–8

 Start or end each bar or strip with half of a pieced block.

When the bars have been sewn, they should be sewn together with the first bar beginning with a half pieced block and the next bar beginning with a whole pieced block. This will stagger the blocks

◼ Hint: *Draw the square on freezer paper. Iron the freezer paper to poster board to make a template.*

so the corner of a block in one row lines up with the center of the long side of a triangle and the intersecting point of two blocks in the previous row. Figure 5–8 shows how to line up two bars for sewing.

OCTAGONAL SET

Eight-sided blocks are used in the Octagonal set. This set was used from around 1850 until today. An octagon is a good choice for plain blocks for fancy quilting and for appliqué blocks. These will look best if framed before setting the blocks together. A few of the blocks that require an Octagonal set are Wedding Ring Tile, Periwinkle, Dove in the Window, Colonial Garden, and Job's Trouble.

Worksheet: Octagonal Set, page 31.

Size of Quilt Top: Measure an octagon block from straight side to straight side.

_____ x _____ = _____
finished octagon   # of blocks   **quilt width**
block width   across

_____ x _____ = _____
finished octagon   # of blocks   **quilt length**
block length   down

Pattern Drafting: To draw an octagon-shaped block, draw a square on a large piece of paper two to three inches larger than the finished size of the block. Using a ruler, draw a long line vertically down the center of the square and another line horizontally across the center of the square (Fig. 6–1).

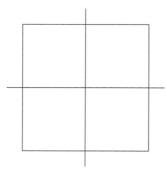

Fig. 6–1

Next, draw lines diagonally from the upper corners to the lower corners, making an X (Fig. 6–2).

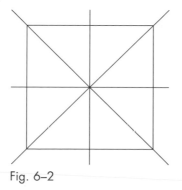

Fig. 6–2

Photo 10. Detail, IN THE HEART OF EUROPE by Margaret Heinisch. Octagonal set. Photo by maker.

The square should now be divided into eight equal parts, which is the number of equal sides needed for the block.

To make an octagon-shaped block the desired size, place the ruler with one–inch markers touching two

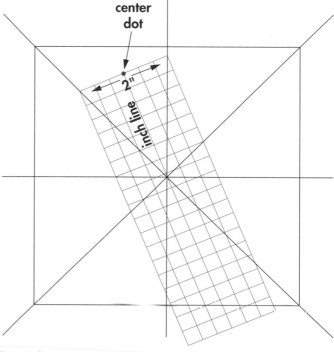

Fig. 6–3

of the lines, a line marker placed exactly on the center (where all of the lines intersect), and measuring 2" between the lines (Fig. 6–3). Make a dot at the center of the ruler where it measures an equal distance between two of the drawn lines. Repeat making center dots in all the spaces between lines.

To make the octagon block, divide the size desired by 2, which, for this example, will be an 8" octagon. Place the ruler with the inch line mark for this number (4 in example) touching the center (where all the lines intersect) and this same measurement on the ruler touching the dot that locates the center between two of the 45° lines. Draw a line along the end of the ruler (Fig. 6–4). Repeat for each of the spaces. The octagon should now look like in Figure 6–5 and should measure from flat side to flat side the size wanted (8" wide, in the example).

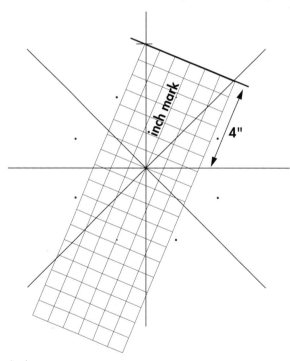

Fig. 6–4

Note that the outside lines of the octagon exactly cross with the 45° angle lines. If they do not cross properly, check the lines and fix them.

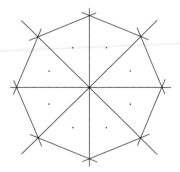

Fig. 6–5

Add seam allowances to all eight sides of the octagon block if it will be used as a plain block or continue drafting the desired pattern inside the octagon.

A setting square will be needed to connect the octagonal-shaped blocks. Measure from angle to angle (Fig. 6–6) to determine the size square needed. Add ½" seam allowances and cut squares this size.

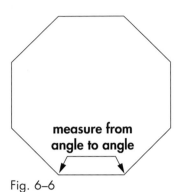

measure from angle to angle

Fig. 6–6

If octagonal blocks will be framed, add the width of the framing piece to the size of the octagon block before determining the size of the setting square.

If the quilt is to have a straight edge, half-square triangles will be needed for the sides/ends and quarter-square triangles for the corners. To **draft the pattern** for the side/end triangles:

$$\frac{\rule{4cm}{0.4pt}}{\text{finished setting square size}} + \tfrac{7}{8}" = \frac{\rule{4cm}{0.4pt}}{\textbf{size of square to draft}}$$

Draw a line diagonally from a lower corner to the opposite upper corner on the drafted square to form two triangles (Fig. 6–7). The triangles now have the seam allowances added and can be used for the pattern to cut triangles for the sides/ends.

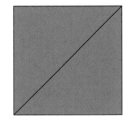

Fig. 6–7

The side/end triangles must be cut with the long side triangle on the straight grain of the fabric to avoid stretching the quilt edges (Fig. 6–8).

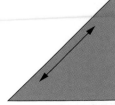

Fig. 6–8

To find the **size to draft the pattern** for the small corner triangles:

$$\frac{}{\text{finished setting square size}} + 1\frac{1}{4}" = \frac{}{\textbf{size of square to draft}}$$

Draw the square on freezer paper. Mark lines diagonally from upper corners to lowers to make a pattern like the one in Figure 6–9. The pattern now has the seam allowances added. Cut the pattern along the diagonal lines and, if drawn on

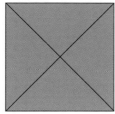

Fig. 6–9

freezer paper, iron to the wrong side of the fabric with the straight grain of the fabric as marked in Figure 6–9. Use a rotary cutter or scissors to cut along the pattern edge.

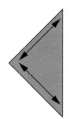 The small corner triangles must be cut with the right angle on the straight of grain of the fabric (Fig. 6–10).

Fig. 6–10

Sewing: Stitch two octagonal blocks together (Fig. 6–11). A setting square should now be sewn to the adjacent sides of two blocks (Fig. 6–12) to make a unit (Fig. 6–13). Stitch only to the seam allowance in the corners of the square and to the

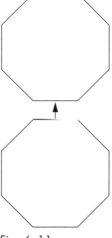

Fig. 6–11

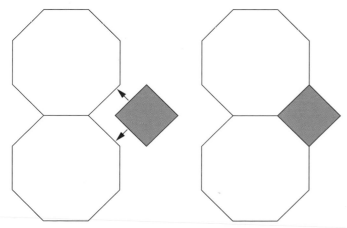

Fig. 6–12   Fig. 6–13

angle on the octagonal block. By not stitching into the seam allowances, the seam allowances of the octagonal blocks can all be pressed outward.

Sew several units; then join the units (Fig. 6–14) until the whole top is constructed.

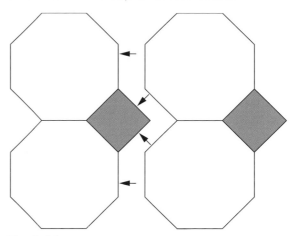

Fig. 6–14

MEDALLION SET

The Medallion set consists of a central block or focal point that is surrounded by several borders that can be solid pieces of fabric, blocks, and pieced and/or appliquéd strips. The focal point can be a set of pieced blocks, one large pieced block, or an appliquéd block.

Photo 11. SPIRIT OF BALTIMORE
by Marjorie L. Mahoney. Medallion set.

A Medallion set will go together better if the quilt is first planned on graph paper. See page 5 for planning a quilt on graph paper.

The combinations and variations of Medallion set designs are numerous. See the Bibliography for books for inspiration.

Worksheet: Use the graph paper on page 33 to design your own medallion set.

Size of Quilt Top:

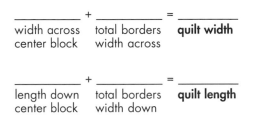

Pattern Drafting: Large triangles used to square up on-point blocks, pieced blocks to fit size of border needed, and other patterns included in the Medallion design may need to be drafted.

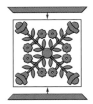

Fig. 7–1

Sewing: The Medallion quilt will be sewn by sewing a border strip to each side of the center (Fig. 7–1), and then to the top and bottom of the center. If, as in the example of a Medallion set (Fig. 7–2), the next part of the quilt is large triangles, those should be sewn next. Continue adding borders in the same way, following the graph paper plan, until all the border units have been added.

OVERALL SET

An Overall set occurs when the pieced design is not finished as a straight–sided block such as the Eight Pointed Star in the example. Rather than finishing the star into a block, it is set together with larger plain blocks, giving spaces for fancy quilting.

Worksheet: Overall Set, page 32.

Size of the Quilt Top:

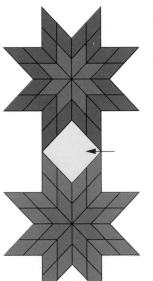

Pattern Drafting: A small square is set in where two points of two stars meet to form a pieced design (Fig. 8–1). To draft the small square, measure the side of a star from one corner of the diamond to the diamond point as shown in Figure 8–2. Add ½" for seam allowances.

Fig. 8–1   Fig. 8–2

Fig. 7–2

🌸 Be sure when measuring that it is the finished size of the pieced design being measured.

Two squares will be needed to join the pieced designs. The size of the large setting square that is used to set four of the pieced designs together is two times the measurement taken for the small square plus ½" for seam allowances (Fig. 8–3).

Fig. 8–3

$$\underset{\text{diamond side measure}}{\underline{\hspace{3cm}}} \times 2 = \underline{\hspace{2cm}} + \tfrac{1}{2}" = \underset{\substack{\textbf{large setting} \\ \textbf{square size}}}{\underline{\hspace{2cm}}}$$

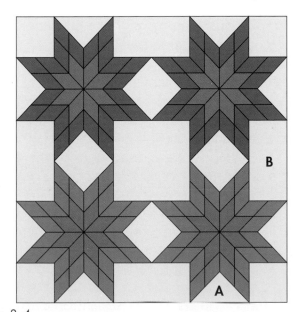

Fig. 8–4

Photo 12. RENAISSANCE by Susan Danielson. Overall set. Photo by maker.

Figure 8–4 shows a half-square triangle (A) and a rectangle (B) that will be needed to finish the quilt top.

To find the **cutting size for the pattern** of the half-square triangle (A):

$$\underset{\text{diamond side measure}}{\underline{\hspace{3cm}}} + \underset{\text{seams}}{\tfrac{7}{8}" \text{ for}} = \underset{\textbf{size of square to draft}}{\underline{\hspace{3cm}}}$$

🌸 This half-square triangle must be cut so the long side of the triangle is on the straight grain of the fabric (Fig. 8–5). ▪

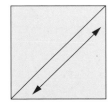

Fig. 8–5

To find the **cutting size of the rectangle** (B):

$$\underset{\text{diamond side measure}}{\underline{\hspace{3cm}}} + \underset{\text{seams}}{\tfrac{1}{2}" \text{ for}} = \underset{\textbf{short side of rectangle}}{\underline{\hspace{3cm}}}$$

$$\underset{\text{diamond side measure}}{\underline{\hspace{3cm}}} \times 2 + \underset{\text{seams}}{\tfrac{1}{2}" \text{ for}} = \underset{\textbf{long side of rectangle}}{\underline{\hspace{3cm}}}$$

Sewing: Sew a small setting square into the pieced design as shown in Figure 8–6. Next, sew another pieced design to the inset square (Fig. 8–7) to make a set. Continue sewing in this manner until all the

▪ **Hint:** Draw the square on freezer paper and use the triangles for patterns by ironing the freezer paper to the fabric and then cutting with either scissors or a rotary cutter.

pieced designs that form the width of the quilt are sewn into rows. Finish the row by sewing the triangles for the side of the quilt to the edge of the pieced design (Fig. 8–8).

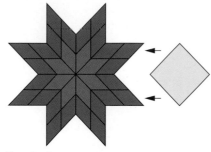

Fig. 8–6

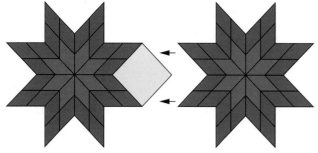

Fig. 8–7

Fig. 8–8

Before sewing the rows together, stitch the small and large squares and rectangles to a row (Fig. 8–9). Add another row of the pieced designs and continue to complete the quilt top. ▪

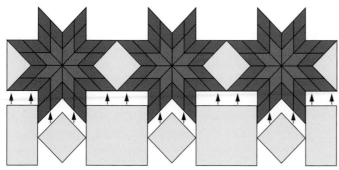

Fig. 8–9

▪ **Hint:** *Although this overall set can be successfully sewn on the machine, it goes together easier if sewn by hand. Pin carefully before sewing.*

RANDOM SET

A Random set is a combination of blocks of many different sizes combined into one quilt top. It is often a sampler of a variety of pieced and/or appliquéd blocks.

Photo 13. MY DAD by Anne Anderberg. Random set. Photo by maker.

Worksheet: Use the graph paper on page 33 to design your own random set.

Size of the Quilt Top: The size of a quilt top with a Random set is best determined by choosing a desired size and then making a graph paper quilt (page 5) for the placement of the blocks.

Decide the width and length you want the quilt to be. Determine what size each square of the graph paper will represent. In Figure 9–1, each square is 2" and this imaginary quilt is 64" wide and 80" long (32 squares x 40 squares). Draw lines on the graph paper to indicate the outside edge of the quilt.

Let's assume a variety of blocks have already been sewn. In order to decide where to place them in a Random set, cut out paper blocks from either construction paper or graph paper to correspond with the finished sizes of the blocks. Use the same scale, in this example 2" per square on the graph

Sets & Sashings for Quilts – Phyllis D. Miller

paper, to make the small blocks. Write the names of the blocks on the paper blocks.

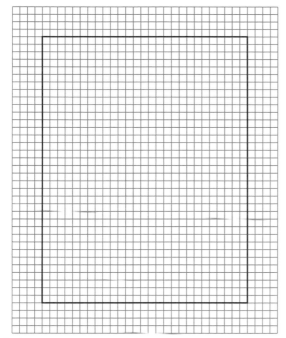

Fig. 9–1

Fig. 9–2

Decide how to arrange the blocks by actually laying them out on the floor, bed, or a wall. When a pleasing arrangement has been found, place the paper blocks on the graph paper quilt in the same arrangement (Fig. 9–2).

The spaces left between blocks on the graph paper quilt indicate where solid strips, framing, pieced strips or appliqué need to be added to fill in between the blocks and complete the quilt top. As you plan the fill-in pieces, look for places where the blocks can be joined into segments that can be sewn together.

Pattern Drafting: Since the fill-in areas are to scale (one square equals 2"), templates or patterns can easily be enlarged to fit. For example, in Figure 9–2, the pattern for the Flying Geese at the lower left hand corner of the paper quilt will need to be drafted to 2" x 4".

Each space between blocks will need to be handled separately. Decide what pattern or design will enhance the blocks and use the graph paper quilt

to count the squares on the graph paper to determine the size of piece needed to fill in the space. Draft the patterns to that size. (Fig. 9–3)

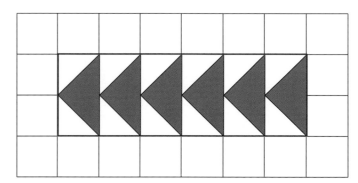

Fig. 9–3

Sewing: Look at the graph paper quilt and decide which blocks can be sewn together in units or sections. Sew the blocks and fill-in pieces together in sections where possible and sew the sections together. Blocks or sections will sometimes need to be set in to complete the quilt top.

UNUSUAL OR UNEXPECTED SET

An Unusual or Unexpected Set is a Random set that has creative block placement, creative sashings to unite the blocks, and creative use of color. The planning directions given could have been used by Karen S. Riggins when she created her quilt, BIRDS OF A FEATHER, shown below. These directions are given to inspire you to try something "unusual". Other books listed in the Bibliography are full of instructions and inspirations for the Unexpected set.

Photo 14. BIRDS OF A FEATHER FLOCK TOGETHER by Karen S. Riggins. Unusual or Unexpected set.

Worksheet: Use the graph paper on page 33 to design your own Unusual or Unexpected set.

Size of the Quilt Top: The size of a quilt top with an Unexpected set can be determined by choosing a finished size first or by the design decisions you make as you create the quilt.

To make a graph paper quilt for an Unusual set, graph paper with 8 squares to the inch is best. You will need 8½" x 11" graph paper for designing and 17" x 22" graph paper for making full-size patterns or templates.

Read about making a paper quilt in the General Instructions section, page 5, first. Decide how many inches each square of the graph paper will represent. Make either little paper blocks or construction paper blocks to use in designing. On a sheet of graph paper, place the squares in a pleasing arrangement. In the example in Figure 10–1, the squares are placed in diagonal rows, or patterned like stairs.

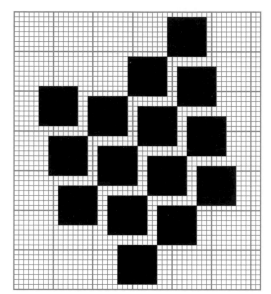

Fig. 10–1

The next step is to draw design lines or lines that connect the blocks (Fig. 10–2). In the example, the blocks appear to be in cubes; this is just one possibility. It will be easier to assemble if the fill-in pieces are a geometric shape. Remember, anything goes!

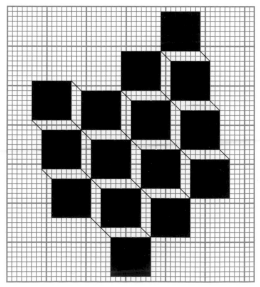

Fig. 10–2

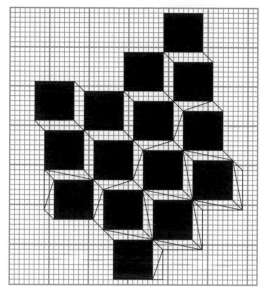

Fig. 10–3

Pattern Drafting: Use the graph paper quilt to transfer the design to the large graph paper sheets. Tape several of the large sheets together, if needed. Transfer the design by counting the squares on the graph paper and multiplying by the inches each square represents. Draw the pattern piece on the large graph paper in the real size. Use a letter/number system to keep up with the position of each piece when sewing. Each pattern piece will need a template. ■

In addition to the cubes, you can create a feeling of birds flying. Add additional design lines to get the illusion of birds in flight (Fig. 10–3) and to add units to frame the outside blocks.

When the graph paper quilt is finished, tracing paper can be placed over the paper quilt and the sashings colored. You may want to make several colorings to explore the possibilities.

Sewing: Look at the design and pick logical units or sections that can be sewn. Refer to the sewing directions for the Random Set on page 23. For example, sew the rhomboid-shaped sashing units first (Fig. 10–4), and then sew the sashing units to the blocks.

Continue sewing pieces and sections together until the quilt top is completed.

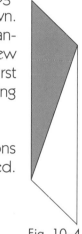

Fig. 10–4

■ *Hint: Sewing is easier if you mark around the template and add the seam allowances as you cut, as you would for hand sewing. Cut each piece of the quilt and place the cut pieces on a design wall as you go. Cut all of the pieces before beginning assembly of the quilt top. A very large quilt could be done in sections.*

WORKSHEETS FOR SETS

Straight Set Worksheet

Sets & Sashings for Quilts – Phyllis D. Miller

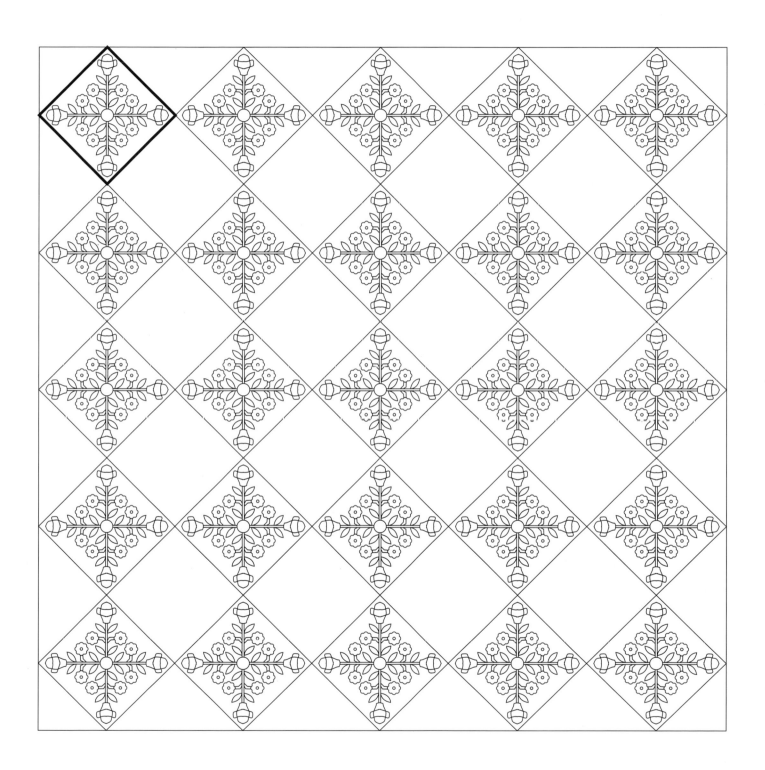

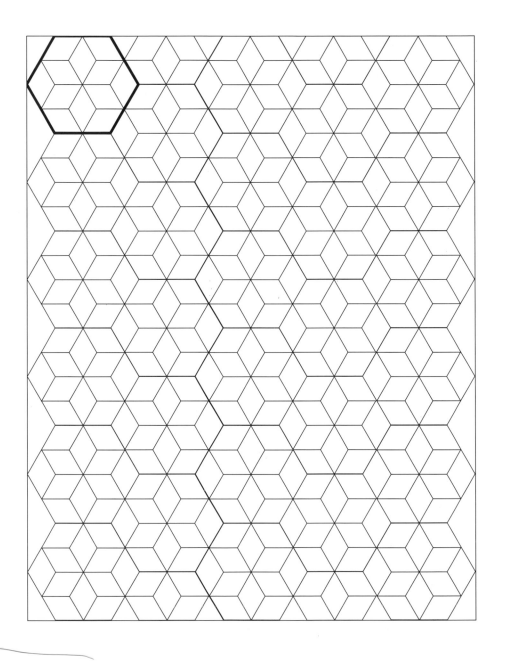

Streak of Lightning Set Worksheet

Use this graph paper for Medallion (page 19), Random (page 22), and Unusual or Unexpected sets (page 24).

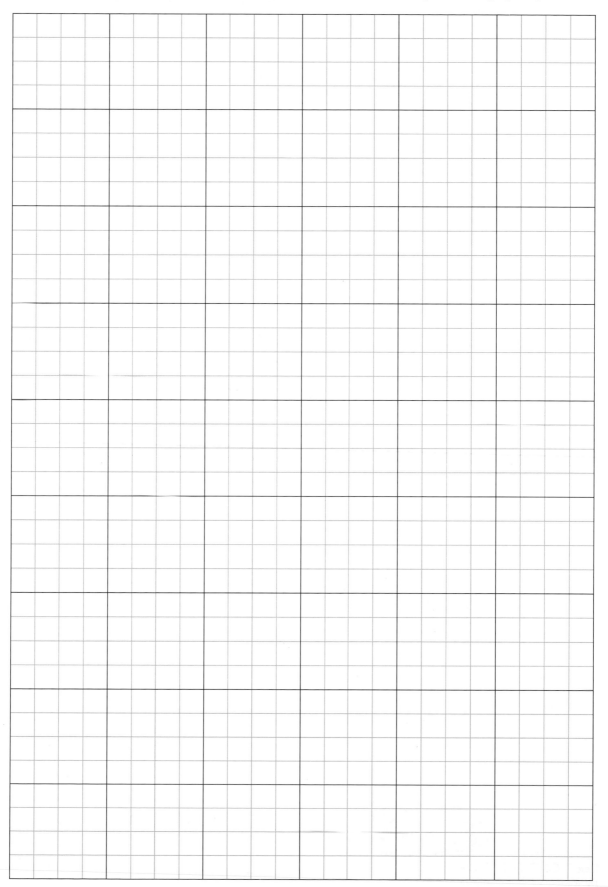

Sets & Sashings for Quilts – Phyllis D. Miller

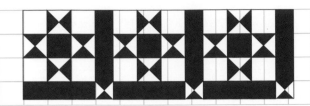

part three
SASHINGS

BLOCKS AS SASHINGS

Blocks used as sashing can be as simple as a plain block, or as elaborate as an appliquéd block. Pieced blocks can add dimension and can create secondary patterns in your quilt.

ALTERNATING PLAIN BLOCKS

This technique involves using solid blocks as sashing. It is also often called Alternating Plain. Pieced and/or appliqué blocks can be set together using plain or solid blocks as sashing. The solid blocks can all be cut from the same fabric or from a variety of fabrics (Photo 15).

Worksheet: Use the graph paper on page 33.

Photo 15. Detail, CARPENTER'S WHEEL by Janice Walden. Alternating Plain blocks.

Setting pieced or appliquéd blocks together with plain blocks is a good way to reduce by half the number of those blocks needed for a quilt top. The plain blocks also allow for more open area to fill with quilting that enhances the quilt.

Solid blocks can be used in Straight, Diagonal, and Bars sets.

Sizing of Sashing: The plain setting blocks will be cut the size of the pieced or appliquéd blocks, plus seam allowances.

$$\underline{} + \frac{1}{2}\text{" for} = \underline{}$$
$$\text{finished pieced/appliqued} \quad \text{seams} \quad \textbf{plain block size}$$
$$\text{block size}$$

Determine the number of plain blocks by making a graph paper quilt (see page 5) or by laying the blocks out on the floor or a bed and counting the number of blocks needed between the pieced or appliquéd blocks.

Cutting: Cut the blocks to size using a rotary cutter. If using a diagonal set, triangles will be needed to fill in the edges of the quilt top. Refer to the Diagonal Set on page 11 for instructions on drafting and cutting the triangles.

Sewing: A quilt top using plain setting blocks will be sewn in the same method as described for a Straight set (page 10), a Diagonal set (page 11), or Bars set (page 14).

ALTERNATING PIECED BLOCKS

Full-size pieced blocks used as sashing add a new dimension and design to both pieced and appliquéd blocks. The pieced blocks for sashing can be as simple as the Snowball block or as complex as a multi-pieced block. The design possibilities are as endless as there are numbers of pieced blocks. Make a graph paper quilt using two different pieced blocks to get an idea of what the blocks

34

Sets & Sashings for Quilts – Phyllis D. Miller

will look like when combined. There are also several computer programs that can be used to experiment with the possibilities. Several simple pieced blocks will be used here to get you started, plus one example using two complex pieced blocks.

ALTERNATING SNOWBALL BLOCK

The Snowball block is a plain square with triangles of another fabric on each of the four corners. The Snowball block enhances a simple Nine-Patch block (Photo 16).

Photo 16. FEEDSACK SNOWBALL
by Mary Sowell. Alternating Snowball blocks.

Combine the Snowball block with another pieced block to use in both Straight and Diagonal sets.

Worksheet: Alternating Snowball Block sashing, page 92.

Sizing of Sashing: The Snowball block must be the same size as the pieced block which, in this example, is a Nine-Patch block.

_____ + ½" for = _____
pieced block size   seams   **size to cut plain fabric block**

The corner triangles for the Snowball block can be sewn by a quick-piecing method using squares. To find the size square needed, measure the finished size of one section or one square of the Nine-Patch.

_____ + ½" for = _____
finished size of one square   seams   **size to cut triangle squares**

Cutting: See the instructions for a plain setting block to determine the number of Snowball blocks needed to make the quilt top the desired size. Cut this number of plain fabric blocks.

Each Snowball block will require four triangles, one for each corner.

_____ x 4 = _____
Snowball blocks needed   **# squares to cut for triangles**

Sewing: With a small ruler and a marking pen or pencil, mark a line diagonally on the small square from corner to corner (Photo 17).

Photo 17.

Lay the small square on a corner of the large square being sure that the corner edges are lined up exactly (Photo 18).

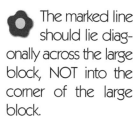 The marked line should lie diagonally across the large block, NOT into the corner of the large block.

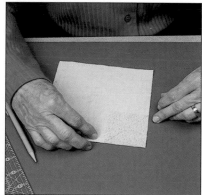

Photo 18.

Next, sew along the marked line diagonally across the small block. Repeat for all four corners. Trim the corner of the large and small blocks, leaving a ¼" seam allowance (Photo 19).

Photo 19.

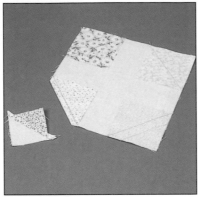

Be sure that the trimming is done toward the corner from the sewing line and NOT toward the center of the block. Press seam allowances toward the darkest fabric.

Alternate the Snowball blocks with the pieced Nine-Patch blocks; sew together into rows, and assemble the rows to complete the quilt top. For a Straight set, see page 10, Diagonal set, page 11, Bars set page 14.

Photo 20. ■ (See hint below.)

ALTERNATING HALF-SQUARE TRIANGLE BLOCKS

This is a simple pieced block that can be used to add a little something extra to both pieced and appliquéd blocks. One half of the block should be a darker color than the other half (Photo 21).

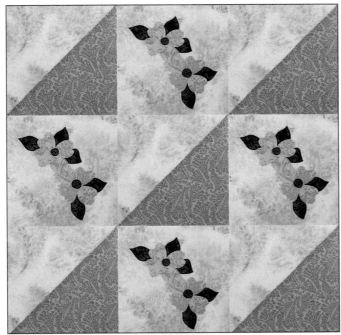

Photo 21. Detail, PINK DOGWOODS
by author. Alternating Half-Square Triangle blocks.

The Half-Square Triangle blocks can be used in either a Straight or Diagonal set.

Worksheet: Alternating Half-Square Triangle Blocks sashing, page 93.

Sizing of Sashing: The Half-Square Triangle block must be the same size as the pieced or appliquéd block.

$$\underline{\hspace{3cm}} + \tfrac{7}{8}" = \underline{\hspace{4cm}}$$

finished block size   **size of square for Half-Square Triangle block**

Cutting: Large Half-Square Triangle blocks can be sewn just like small blocks using a quick sewing method. First, determine the total number Half-Square blocks needed to complete the quilt top by either making a graph paper quilt or laying out the actual blocks and counting the number needed.

To use the quick–sewing method, cut squares of one fabric to total one half the number of the total blocks needed. For example, if 16 Half-Square Triangle blocks will be needed, cut eight full squares from one fabric and the same number (eight) from the other fabric.

Sewing: Lay a long ruler on the lightest fabric with the ruler edge touching one upper corner and the opposite lower corner (Photo 22). With a fabric marking pen or pencil, draw a line diagonally from corner to corner. Place the marked square on top of the darker square with right sides together.

Photo 22.

Sew a seam ¼" from the marked line on one side of the marked line and then on the other side so there are two seams (Photo 23). Using a ruler and a rotary

---

■ **HINT:** *The small triangles that will be cut from the four corners can be sewn together to make small blocks that can be used in other projects. This sewing can be done before cutting the triangles from the large block by sewing ½" from the already sewn line (Photo 20). Cut between the two sewing lines to produce not only the Snowball block but also four half-square triangle blocks. Save these extra half-square blocks to use in another project.*

        Sets & Sashings for Quilts – Phyllis D. Miller

Photo 23.

cutter or scissors, cut along the marked line from corner to corner.

Press the block with the seam allowance going toward the darkest fabric. Trim off triangles tips and the Half-Square Triangle blocks are now ready to be sewn with the pieced or appliquéd blocks into a quilt top.

ALTERNATING QUARTER-SQUARE TRIANGLE BLOCKS

This block composed of four triangles is another simple pieced block that can be combined with other pieced or appliquéd blocks to add a new design to a quilt (Photo 24). ■

Quarter-Square Triangle blocks can be used in both Straight and Diagonal sets.

Worksheet: Alternating Quarter-Square Triangle Blocks Sashing, page 94.

Sizing of Sashing: The Quarter-Square Triangle blocks must be the same size as the pieced or appliqué blocks.

$$\frac{\text{_____}}{\text{finished pieced block size}} + 1\frac{1}{4}" = \frac{\text{_____}}{\text{\textbf{size of square for Quarter-Square blocks}}}$$

Cutting: Large Quarter-Square Triangle blocks can be sewn using a quick sewing method. First, determine how many of these blocks are needed to alternate with the pieced or appliquéd blocks to complete the quilt top.

Each Quarter-Square Triangle block will require two pieces of fabric in either two different colors or one light and one dark fabric. By using a

Photo 24. Detail, AUTUMN SPLENDOR
by author. Alternating Quarter-Square Triangle blocks.

quick–sewing method, two squares (two different fabrics) cut the determined size will produce two Quarter-Square Triangle blocks.

Cut half the number of needed Quarter-Square Triangles blocks from each of the two fabrics. (Example: cut 8 from each fabric to make 16 blocks.)

Sewing: Place two of the different color fabric squares with right sides together. On the lightest of the two fabrics, use a fabric marking pen or pencil to mark a diagonal line from an upper corner to the opposite lower corner (Photo 22).

Sew a seam ¼" from the center marked line on both sides of the marked line. Cut with scissors or a rotary cutter along the marked diagonal line. Press with the seam allowance to the darker fabric. You should now have two Half-Square Triangle blocks.

Using a ruler and a fabric marking pen or pencil, mark a line diagonally from an upper corner to a lower corner on the wrong side of one of the Half-Square Triangle blocks. Place two Half-Square Triangle blocks right sides together with a dark half

■ **Hint:** *Make a graph paper quilt and play with the placement of the Quarter-Square Triangle blocks to see how they are the most pleasing. By arranging the placement of color in the rows, the pieced or appliquéd blocks can appear to be alternately framed by the two colors.*

above a light half (Photo 25). The seam should butt up against a seam snugly. Pin if necessary.

Photo 25.

Sew a seam ¼" from the center marked line on both sides of the marked line (Photo 23). ▪

Cut with scissors or rotary cutter along the center marked line. Open and press.

You have two Quarter-Square Triangle blocks that are ready to be sewn to the pieced or appliquéd blocks into a quilt top.

ALTERNATING TRADITIONAL PIECED BLOCK

The combination of a pieced block set together with different pieced blocks offers endless design possibilities. The setting or sashing block must be the same size as the pieced or appliquéd block. Usually, blocks of the same construction style will work best together. For example, if the block you have is a nine-patch construction, another block based on a nine-patch will work well with it. Make a graph paper quilt and try different block pattern combinations to see what happens.

The quilt in the example (Photo 26) shows the Judy in Arabia block with the Shoo Fly block. A new design appears where the edge of one block touches the edge of the other.

There are also many pieced blocks that will combine with appliquéd blocks to take them from good to extraordinary. The simple combination of a Double Nine-Patch with an appliquéd block makes a big difference in the excitement of the quilt.

Use a Traditional Pieced Block as sashing in a Straight, Diagonal, or Bars set.

Worksheets: Alternating Traditional Pieced Block sashing, page 95 and Alternating Appliquéd Blocks with Pieced Block sashing, page 96.

Photo 26. Detail, JUDY, DORIS, AND THE DEVIL by author. Alternating Traditional Pieced blocks.

Sewing: Refer to the sewing instructions on page 10 for a Straight set, page 11 for a Diagonal set, and page 14 for the Bars set.

STRIP SASHING

Sashings can also be made from strips of fabric. These strips can be of a single plain fabric or several strips sewn together, or combined with connecting blocks.

PLAIN STRIP

Plain strip sashing refers to strips of fabric that divide or separate blocks from each other. Plain strip sashing can be the same fabric as the background of the blocks or it can be a complementary color that will accent or highlight the blocks. This sashing can be used in a Straight, Diagonal, Bars, Hexagonal, or Octagonal sets (Photo 27).

▪ *Hint:* *If you cannot adjust your machine needle to sew ¼" seams or do not have a foot that measures ¼" from the needle, use a ruler to mark the stitching lines ¼" on both sides of the already marked line. These lines will be your sewing lines.*

Photo 27. Detail, WILD ABOUT WILDFLOWERS III
by Beatrice S. Oglesby. Plain Strip sashing.
Photo by maker.

Sizing of Sashing: The width of the sashing can be whatever is desired. A guideline in beginning is to use the width of one section of the block or ¼ to ⅓ of the entire block width. (For example, a Nine-Patch has three sections; use ⅓ of the block width.)

Worksheet: Plain Strip sashing, page 97.

÷ ¼ or ⅓ =	+ ½" for =
block width	finished sashing width	seams	**width to cut sashing**

+ ½" for seams =
block length	**length to cut sashing**

×	+	×	=
block width	# of blocks	sashing width	# sashing strips

length to cut sashing strip to go across quilt top between rows

Cutting: To rotary cut the sashing strips, cut across the fabric width (selvage to selvage) making a strip that is as wide as the length of the sashing. Cut this wide strip lengthwise in strips the width of the

sashing to make as many plain sashing strips as needed for the quilt top.

Sewing: Sew a sashing strip to one side of each block (Fig. 11–1). Sew these block/sashing units into rows (Fig. 11–2). Add a sashing strip to the end of the row, if needed, or leave the last block without a sashing strip.

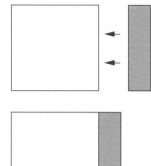

Sew a long sashing strip to a row of blocks by placing the right sides of the block

Fig. 11–1

row and sashing strip together (Fig. 11–3). Add another row of block/sashing units (Fig. 11–4), and then a long sashing strip, and continue sewing in the same sequence until the quilt top is complete.

Fig. 11–2

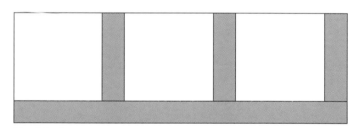

Fig. 11–3

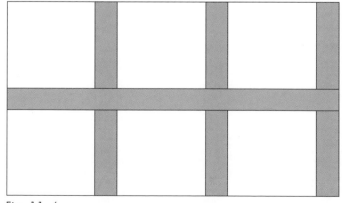

Fig. 11–4

PLAIN STRIP WITH CONNECTING BLOCKS

One way to add another dimension to a simple single sashing is to connect the sashing strips at block corners with a small block. This connecting block can be a plain block or a pieced block.

Photo 28. Detail, NEW HOUSE, NEW ROOM, NEW QUILT by Eileen B. Sullivan. Plain Strip with Connecting Blocks sashing.

This sashing can be used in a Straight set, Diagonal set (Photo 28), and a Hexagonal set.

Worksheet: Use the Plain Strip (page 97) and add connecting blocks by drawing lines with a ruler.

Sizing of Sashing: Read about the sizing of Plain Strip sashing on page 39 to decide what width and length the sashing strips will be.

$\underline{}$	$\div$ ¼ or ⅓ =	$\underline{}$	+ ½" for = seams	$\underline{}$
block width		finished sashing width		**width to cut sashing**

$\underline{}$	+ ½" for =	$\underline{}$
block length	seams	**length to cut sashing**

$\underline{}$	=	$\underline{}$
width to cut sashing		**size to cut connecting square**

Cutting: Follow the instructions for cutting the plain sashing strips on page 39. To rotary cut the connecting squares, cut a strip across the width of the fabric the size needed for the connecting square. Cut this strip into squares.

Sewing: Assemble the blocks and plain sashing strips in rows as described on page 39. To sew the strip that goes across the quilt top between the rows with the blocks, assemble a row by placing a plain sashing strip with the length going across, then a connecting block and so forth. There should be a sashing strip for the bottom of each block (Fig. 11–5). Sew this row strip by placing the sashing strip and the connecting block right sides together (Fig. 11–6), and sew the block to the strip. Sew another strip to this unit, and then another block. Continue until the row is the same length as the block/sashing strip (Fig. 11–5).

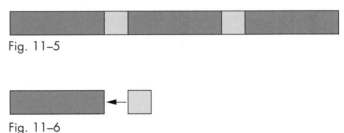

Fig. 11–5

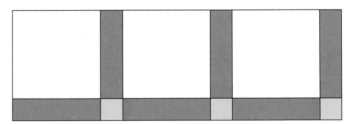

Fig. 11–6

To assemble the quilt top, place a block/sashing strip right sides together with a connecting block/sashing row (Fig. 11–7).

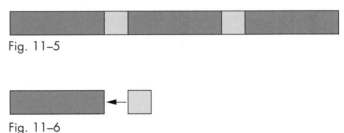

Fig. 11–7

Sew these two row units together. Continue sewing block/sashing rows and connecting block/sashing strips in the same order until the quilt top is complete. One connecting block/sashing strip needs to be added at the top edge if the sashing is to go completely around the edges of the quilt.

PLAIN STRIP WITH PIECED CONNECTING BLOCKS

A simple Quarter-Square Triangle block can give a new look to plain strip sashing (Photo 29).

Photo 29. Detail, BASKETS by the author.
Plain Strip with Pieced Connecting Blocks sashing.

Worksheet: Plain Strip with Pieced Connecting Blocks sashing, page 98.

Sizing of Sashing: The plain sashing strip size is determined in the same method as used for the plain strip sashing with connecting blocks on page 39. The pieced connecting blocks must finish the same size as the width of the sashing strips.

$$\underline{\hspace{4cm}} + 1\frac{1}{4}" = \underline{\hspace{4cm}}$$
sashing strip finished size   **size of fabric squares to cut**

Cutting: To make the pieced Quarter-Square Triangle connecting block using a quick-piecing method, each block will require two pieces of fabric in either different colors or values. One color should be the same fabric as the sashing strip and another fabric that is either darker, lighter, or the same as the block background fabric.

Determine how many connecting blocks will be needed. Each set of two fabric squares will produce two Quarter-Square Triangle blocks. Divide the number of connecting blocks by two. This is

the number of squares of each of the two fabrics that will need to be cut.

Sewing: Place two of the different color fabric squares with right sides together. On the lightest of the two fabrics, use a fabric marking pen or pencil to mark a diagonal line from an upper corner to the lower opposite corner. See page 37 for instructions for construction of Quarter-Square Triangle blocks.

Sew a seam ¼" from the center marked line on both sides of the marked line. Cut with scissors or a rotary cutter along the marked diagonal line. Press the seam allowances toward the darker fabric. You should have two Half-Square Triangle blocks.

Using a ruler and a fabric marking pen or pencil, mark a line diagonally from an upper corner to a lower corner on the wrong side of one of the Half-Square Triangle blocks. Place the two Half-Square Triangle blocks right sides together with a dark half on top of a light half. The seams should butt up against against each other. Pin, if necessary.

Sew a seam ¼" from the center marked line on both sides of the marked line. Cut with scissors or rotary cutter along the center marked line. Open and press. You should have two Quarter-Square Triangle blocks that are ready to be used as connecting blocks with the sashing strips (Fig. 11–8).

Fig. 11–8

Assemble the blocks and sashing strips into a row (Fig. 11–9). Assemble a row of sashing strips and connecting Quarter-Square Triangle blocks (Fig. 11–10). Pin the block/sashing strip row and the connecting block, right sides together, at the seams and sew (Fig. 11–11). Add another row of blocks/sashing strips, then sashing strips/connecting blocks until the quilt top is complete.

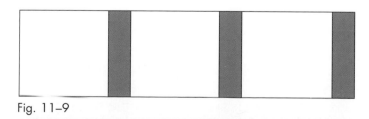

Fig. 11–9

Fig. 11–10

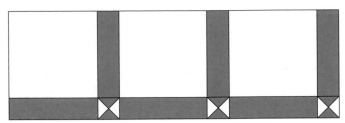

Fig. 11–11

MULTIPLE STRIP SASHING

A multiple strip sashing has two or more fabric strips sewn together to make a sashing strip unit. These multiple strip sashing units have complimentary pieced connecting blocks.

DOUBLE STRIP

This sashing has two different fabrics, one lighter or darker than the other. The Double Strips sashing has a four-patch block for the connecting blocks. This simple sashing makes a quilt more interesting as the two fabrics frame alternate blocks (Photo 30).

Photo 30. Detail, WORTH THEIR WEIGHT IN GOLD. Block by Marie Salazar. Double Strip sashing

Worksheet: Double Strip sashing, page 99.

Sizing of Sashing: The double sashing can be narrow to wide. A good choice for the size of the double strip is ¼ to ⅓ of a section of the block that the sashing will be used with. Each fabric will be one half of the desired width of the sashing strip. Decide how wide the double strip sashing will be.

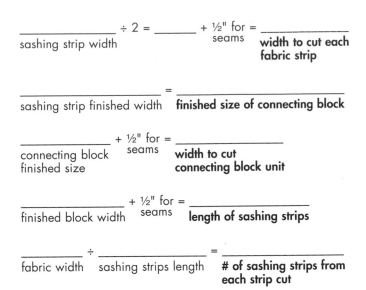

$\underline{\hspace{3cm}} \div 2 = \underline{\hspace{2cm}} + \frac{1}{2}\text{" for} = \underline{\hspace{3cm}}$
sashing strip width   seams   **width to cut each fabric strip**

$\underline{\hspace{3cm}} = \underline{\hspace{3cm}}$
sashing strip finished width   **finished size of connecting block**

$\underline{\hspace{3cm}} + \frac{1}{2}\text{" for} = \underline{\hspace{3cm}}$
connecting block   seams   **width to cut**
finished size   **connecting block unit**

$\underline{\hspace{3cm}} + \frac{1}{2}\text{" for} = \underline{\hspace{3cm}}$
finished block width   seams   **length of sashing strips**

$\underline{\hspace{2cm}} \div \underline{\hspace{3cm}} = \underline{\hspace{3cm}}$
fabric width   sashing strips length   **# of sashing strips from each strip cut**

Cutting: Across the fabric grain, from selvage to selvage, cut strips the width determined for each fabric strip. Cut enough strips to get the number of sashing strips needed plus one extra strip to use in making the connecting blocks.

Sewing: Place the two different long fabric strips, right sides together, and sew. Cut these sewn strips to the lengths needed for the sashing strips. Sew and cut as many of these double-sashing units as needed for the quilt top (Photo 31).

Photo 31.

Take one of the long sewn double strips and cut it into sections the width of the connecting unit (Photo 32). Place two of the connecting units with right sides together, a dark section against a light section.

Photo 32.

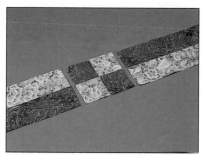

Photo 33.

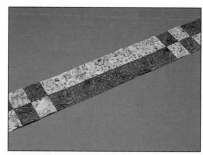

Photo 34.

Photo 35.

Sew these two units together to make a four-patch connecting block (Photo 33).

Form a row by placing a block, double sashing unit, connecting block, etc. to make a row as wide as needed for the quilt top (Photo 34). Notice that the placement of the dark side of the double sashing strip and the light/dark orientation of the connecting block will alternate as you move across the row. The next row will be a double sashing unit, a four-patch block, etc., to make a row as wide as the block row (Photo 35).

Finish sewing rows of blocks/sashing and rows of sashing/four-patch connecting blocks to finish the quilt top.

When sewing, be sure to watch the light/dark placement of the sashing strips and connecting blocks so the light fabric is always touching dark fabric. Being careful as you go eliminates ripping seams.

TRIPLE STRIP

The triple strip sashing has two different fabrics, one dark and one light. The placement of the dark and light fabric is personal preference. The triple strip sashing illustrated uses dark outer strips and a light fabric between. The connecting block for the triple strip sashing is a Nine-Patch block. This first triple sashing will be described using three equal width strips (Photo 36).

Photo 36. Detail, EASTERN STARS by the author. Triple Strip sashing.

Worksheet: Triple Strip sashing, page 100.

Sizing of Sashing: For ease in figuring, make the width of this sashing a number that is evenly divided by 3. A 3" triple strip sashing is a good choice.

_____ ÷ 3 = _____ + ½" for = _____
sashing strip width   seams   **width to cut each fabric strip**

_____ = _____
sashing strip finished width   **connecting block finished size**

_____ + ½" for = _____
connecting block   seams
finished size   **width to cut connecting block unit**

_____ + ½" for = _____
finished block width   seams   **length of sashing strips**

_____ ÷ _____ = _____
fabric width   sashing strips length   **# of sashing strips from each light strip**

_____ ÷ _____ x 2 = _____
fabric width   sashing length   **# of sashing strips from each dark strip**

Cutting: Across the grain of the light fabric, from selvage to selvage, cut strips the width determined for the fabric strips. Cut enough strips to get the number of sashing strips plus one extra strip to make the Nine-Patch connecting block.

Cut strips from the dark fabric in the same manner. Remember that the dark fabric is used two times in the triple strip sashing so twice as many strips must be cut. Cut one extra strip of dark fabric to make the Nine-Patch blocks.

Sewing: Sew together three strips of fabric in dark/light/dark order (Photo 37). Sew together enough of these three fabric units to make the number of triple strip sashings needed to complete the quilt top. Cut the sewn sashing units the required sashing length. Cut the leftovers in unit widths to make the Nine-Patch connecting blocks. One fabric strip width of the sewn sashing unit is needed for each connecting block.

Photo 37.

Sew together another set of three strips of fabric. This time the fabric placement should be light, dark and then a light strip (Photo 38). Cut two connecting units from this triple strip for each Nine-Patch block needed.

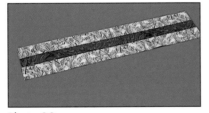
Photo 38.

Sew the three sets of connecting units together to make a Nine-Patch block as shown in Photo 39.

Photo 39.

To assemble the quilt top, sew together a row made up of a block, triple strip sashing, block, etc. in the quilt width desired (Photo 40).

Photo 40.

Next, sew together another row that is triple strip sashing, Nine-Patch connecting block, etc. to obtain the same width as the block row (Photo 41). Sew the rows together to form the completed quilt top.

Photo 41.

UNEQUAL TRIPLE STRIP

In this variation of Triple Strip sashing, two strips are one width and the third is either wider or narrower. In this example, the middle strip of the sashing is light and wide and the two outside strips are dark and narrow. The connecting block for this Unequal Triple Strip sashing is an Unequal Nine-Patch block, also called Counterpane (Photo 42).

Photo 42. Detail, VIVACIOUS FLOWERS.
Blocks by Marie Salazar. Unequal Triple Strip sashing.

Worksheet: Unequal Triple Strip sashing, page 101.

Sizing of Sashing: For this example, the finished width of the sashing unit is 4 inches. The dark narrow strips will be ¾" wide finished and the wide light strip will be 2½" wide.

	+ ½" for =	
dark strip width	seams	**width to cut narrow fabric strips**

	+ ½" for =	
light strip width	seams	**width to cut wide fabric strips**

_____ = _____
width to cut narrow   **width to cut light strips**
fabric strips   **for connecting blocks**

_____ = _____
width of wide   **width to cut dark strips**
fabric strips   **for connecting blocks**

_____ = _____
# connecting blocks needed   **# large sections to cut**

_____ = _____
width to cut wide   **width to cut large sections**
fabric strips   **for connecting blocks**

_____ = _____
width to cut narrow   **width to cut rectangle sections**
fabric strips   **for connecting blocks**

_____ x 2 = _____
connecting blocks needed   **# rectangle sections to cut**

_____ = _____
sashing strip finished width   **connecting block finished size**

_____ + ½" for = _____
finished block width   seams   **length of sashing strips**

Cutting: Photo 43 shows the dark/light arrangement for the Unequal Triple Strip sashing.

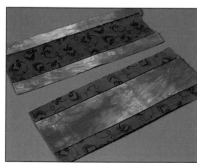

Cut strips across the grain of the dark fabric, selvage to selvage, the width for the narrow strips. Cut the light fabric the width for the middle strips.

Photo 43.

For the connecting blocks, cut two strips from the light fabric the width of the narrow strips. Cut one strip the width of the wide strips from the dark fabric.

Sewing: Arrange the strips in a narrow dark, wide light, narrow dark order. Sew the strips together and press the seam allowances toward the dark fabric. From these triple strip pieces, cut units the length of the sashing strips to make the number of sashing strips needed for the quilt top.

For the connecting block, sew another group of fabric strips in the same sequence (dark/light/dark) as for the sashing units. Cut sections the width of the wide fabric strips. Sew another strip with the light/dark/light arrangement. Cut this strip into the width of the narrow fabric strips.

To sew the connecting block, lay out the units (Photo 44). Sew these together to make Unequal Nine-Patch or Counterpane connecting blocks.

Sew the blocks and sashing and connecting blocks together in rows as shown for the Triple Strip sashing on page 43. Complete the quilt top by sewing the rows together.

Photo 44.

GARDEN MAZE

Garden Maze is a multiple strip sashing with a pieced connecting block. The sashing strips for the Garden Maze are made like the Unequal Triple Strip sashing with the center strip being wider than the two outside strips. The connecting block is an X with strips that appear to go over and under each other to make this sashing rise above the ordinary (Photo 45).

Photo 45. Detail, STARS IN THE GARDEN by author. Garden Maze sashing.

The Garden Maze sashing can be used with sampler blocks, appliquéd blocks, or pieced blocks. It can be used with either a straight or diagonal set. This sashing is visually very pleasing and is not difficult to sew.

Pattern: Page 47 has the pattern for a 6" wide Garden Maze connecting block.

Worksheet: Garden Maze sashing, page 102.

Sizing of Sashing: The most often used width for the Garden Maze sashing is 6". The outside strips should be narrower than the center strip. A pleasing combination is a finished width of 1½" inches for the outer or dark strips and 3" finished for the center or light strip.

_____ + ½" for = _____
finished width of dark strips   seams   **width to cut dark fabric strips**

_____ + ½" for = _____
finished width of light strips   seams   **width to cut light fabric strips**

_____ + ½" for = _____
finished block width   seams   **length to cut sashing strips**

Drafting: To make your own pattern for the connecting block and sashing in a different width than 6", substitute the sashing widths that you desire as you follow the instructions for drafting the connecting block.

Draw two 6" blocks side by side on plain or graph paper. In one of the 6" blocks, draw a line 1½" from the top and another line 1½" from the bottom of the 6" square (Fig. 11–12).

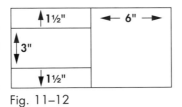
Fig. 11–12

In the blank block on the paper, make a dot that indicates the width of the narrow strip or 1½" from the sides of the square. Do this on all 4 sides (Fig. 11–13). With a ruler, draw diagonal lines from dot to dot (Fig. 11–14).

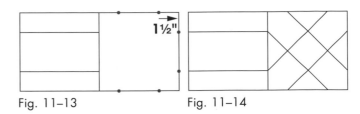
Fig. 11–13   Fig. 11–14

To make the connecting block easier to sew or with fewer pieces, erase the crossover lines (Fig. 11–15). Mark the pieces A, B, C (Fig. 11–15). The graph paper drawing is now ready for making templates by adding ¼" seam allowances to all sides of the pattern units.

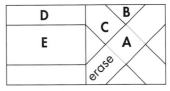
Fig. 11–15

Cutting: For each connecting block:
- cut 1 A piece from the dark fabric
- cut 4 B pieces from the light fabric
- cut 2 C pieces from the dark fabric

_____ = _____
# connecting blocks needed   **# piece A to cut**

_____ x 4 = _____
connecting blocks needed   **# piece B to cut**

_____ x 2 = _____
connecting blocks needed   **# piece C to cut**

Sewing: Arrange the strips of fabric for the sashing units in a dark, light, dark arrangement. Sew these strips together. Press the seam allowances toward the dark fabric. From these triple strip pieces, cut sashing units in the length and number needed for the quilt top.

To piece the connecting blocks, sew a piece B to each side of Piece C (Fig. 11–16); make two units for each block. Sew these units to each side of piece A (Fig. 11–17). The finished connecting block should look like the one in Figure 11–18.

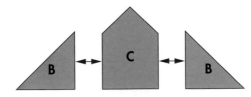
Fig. 11–16

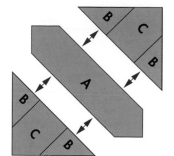

Fig. 11–17

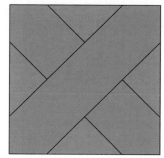

Fig. 11–18

To sew the parts of the Garden Maze into a quilt top, make a row with an X block, sashing strip, X block, etc. Sew as many of these units together as needed to make the row the width of the quilt top. Next, sew the sashing strips/plain, pieced or appliquéd blocks/sashing strips, etc. to the desired width. Sew these two rows together (Fig. 11–19) and continue adding rows in the same sequence until the quilt top is finished.

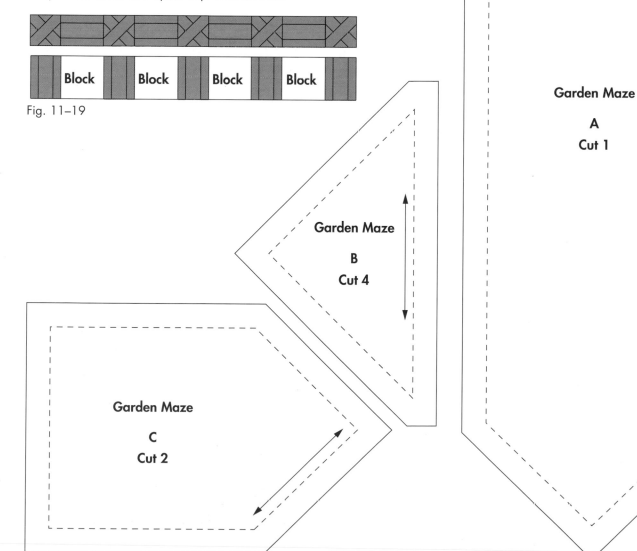

Fig. 11–19

Garden Maze

A

Cut 1

Garden Maze

B

Cut 4

Garden Maze

C

Cut 2

SASHING FROM TRADITIONAL PIECED BLOCKS

Traditional pieced blocks are an endless source of inspiration that can be used as sashing between blocks. Look at the center sections of pieced blocks and see if a part of the block can be used for sashing. Five traditional blocks with the sections highlighted that could be used for sashing are shown in Figure 12–1.

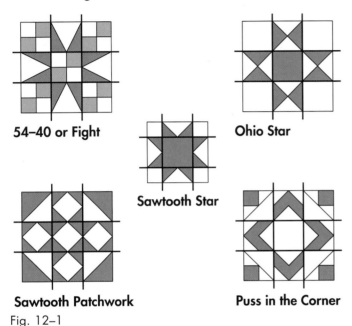

54–40 or Fight

Ohio Star

Sawtooth Star

Sawtooth Patchwork

Puss in the Corner

Fig. 12–1

SAWTOOTH STAR

This simple, traditional pieced block would be a good sashing choice for a quilt with a theme that stars would enhance, such as Christmas quilts, patriotic quilts, and quilts made for a male. The connecting square and the triangles that make the Sawtooth Star can be all the same color or the square can be one color and the triangles another (Photo 46).

Pattern: Sawtooth Star sashing, 3" wide and 12" long, page 126.

Worksheet: Sawtooth Star sashing, page 103.

Sizing of Sashing: The size of a Sawtooth Star sashing would be determined by how prominent you wish the stars to be. Since the traditional block is a four-patch block, the width of the sashing should be divisible by two. For example: 2" width ÷ 2 = 1; 3" width ÷ 2 = 1½; 4" width ÷ 2 = 2.

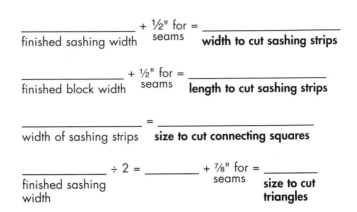

$$\underline{\hspace{3cm}} + \frac{1}{2}" \text{ for } = \underline{\hspace{3cm}}$$
finished sashing width   seams   **width to cut sashing strips**

$$\underline{\hspace{3cm}} + \frac{1}{2}" \text{ for } = \underline{\hspace{3cm}}$$
finished block width   seams   **length to cut sashing strips**

$$\underline{\hspace{3cm}} = \underline{\hspace{3cm}}$$
width of sashing strips   **size to cut connecting squares**

$$\underline{\hspace{3cm}} \div 2 = \underline{\hspace{2cm}} + \frac{7}{8}" \text{ for } = \underline{\hspace{2cm}}$$
finished sashing width   seams   **size to cut triangles**

Drafting: For illustration purposes, the directions show a 4" wide sashing for a 12" block. On a piece of paper longer than the length of the sashing, draw a line the length of the sashing (12"). Measure down from this line the width of the sashing (4") and draw another line the length of the sashing. Draw lines across the ends to make a rectangle that is the size of the finished sashing (Fig. 12–2).

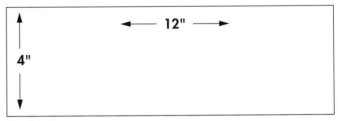

Fig. 12–2

Divide the finished width (4") of the sashing by two. Mark this distance (2") from both ends of the paper rectangle; mark the center of the ends of the rectangle (Fig. 12–3).

Fig. 12–3

Draw lines from the center end mark to the marks on the sides of the rectangle (Fig. 12–4).

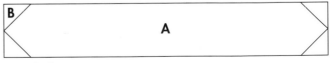

Fig. 12–4

The drafted patterns are now ready to use by adding ¼" seam allowances to all sides to make templates.

The connecting square for the drafted Sawtooth Star is the width of the sashing (4") plus ½" for seam allowances. The connecting squares should be cut in 4½" squares.

Cutting: Determine the number of sashing units and connecting blocks needed by making a paper quilt (see page 5). For each sashing unit, cut four of pattern piece B and one of pattern piece A. Cut one (1) connecting square for each sashing intersection.

_____ = _____
# sashing units needed   # piece A to cut

_____ x 4 = _____
sashing units needed   # piece B to cut

_____ = _____
# connecting blocks needed   # connecting blocks to cut

Sewing: Sew pieces B to one end of the sashing piece A (Fig. 12–5). Press. Repeat by sewing pieces B to the other end of the sashing piece A.

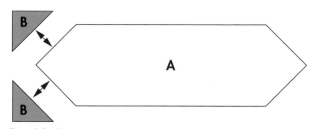

Fig. 12–5

Alternate blocks with sashing units to make a row the desired quilt top width (Fig. 12–6).

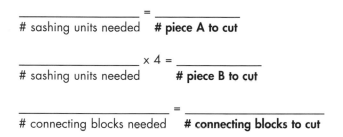

Fig. 12–6

Photo 46. DUSK TIL DAWN
by Debbie H. Barber. Ohio Star sashing.
Photo by maker.

Sew sashing units together with connecting squares (C) in strips to go across the quilt (Fig. 12–7). Assemble the quilt top by sewing a row of blocks/sashing units to a row of sashing units/connecting blocks (Fig. 12–8).

Fig. 12–7

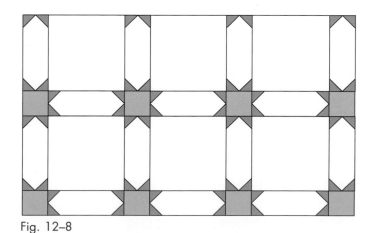

Fig. 12–8

54-40 OR FIGHT

The sharp triangles in this pieced block add a good secondary design to a quilt top when used as sashing. The center of the block or the connecting block can be changed from the four-patch block in the 54-40 or Fight block to a quarter-square triangle block, solid square or a square on-point block (Fig. 12-9) (Photo 47).

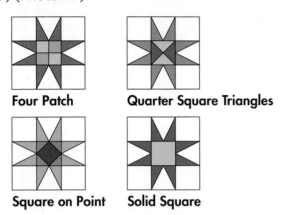

Four Patch   **Quarter Square Triangles**

Square on Point   **Solid Square**

Fig. 12–9

Pattern: 54-40 or Fight sashing, 4" wide and 12" long - page 127.

Worksheet: 54-40 or Fight sashing, page 104.

Sizing of Sashing: Determine the width of the sashing by deciding how prominent you wish the secondary design to be. The width of the sashing can be small or large depending on the size of the quilt blocks. Since the base on the long triangles is one half of the block section, the width of the sashing should be divisible by 2.

_____ + ½" for = _____
finished sashing width   seams   **width to cut sashing**

_____ ÷ 2 + ½" for = _____
sashing width   seams   **size to cut squares for Four-Patch connecting block**

_____ = _____
width of sashing strips   **finished size of connecting blocks**

Drafting: For illustration purposes, the sashing is 3" wide and 12" long. On plain or graph paper, draw a 3" wide x 12" long rectangle (Fig. 12–10).

Draw a square the width of the sashing on one end of the rectangle and mark the center of the end of that square (Fig. 12–11). Using a ruler, draw a line from the center mark to the upper corner of the square and from the center mark to the lower corner of the square (Fig. 12–12). Add ¼" seam allowances to all sides of the long triangles to make two templates, A and Reverse A (Fig. 12–13). Repeat the drawing of the square and marking the triangles on the other end of the rectangle and add ¼" seam allowances to all sides to make template (B) for the sashing (Fig. 12–14). ■

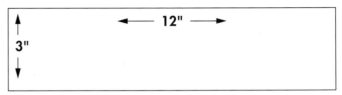

Fig. 12–10

Fig. 12–11

Fig. 12–12

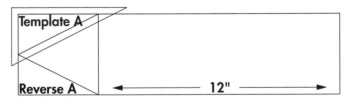

Fig. 12–13

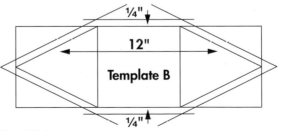

Fig. 12–14

■ *Hint: Do not cut off the points of the templates. It is easier to match up the points and sew them together if the sharp points are left on.*

Cutting: For each connecting block, cut two of pattern piece A and two of pattern piece Reverse A. For each connecting square, cut two squares from dark fabric and two from light fabric. Use pattern piece B to cut the number of sashing strips that are needed.

$$\frac{\rule{3cm}{0.4pt}}{\text{\# sashing units needed}} = \frac{\rule{2cm}{0.4pt}}{\text{\# piece B to cut}}$$

$$\frac{\rule{3cm}{0.4pt}}{\text{\# sashing units needed}} \times 2 = \frac{\rule{2cm}{0.4pt}}{\text{\# piece A to cut}}$$

$$\frac{\rule{3cm}{0.4pt}}{\text{\# sashing units needed}} \times 2 = \frac{\rule{2cm}{0.4pt}}{\text{\# piece Reverse A to cut}}$$

$$\frac{\rule{3cm}{0.4pt}}{\text{\# connecting squares needed}} \times 2 = \frac{\rule{2cm}{0.4pt}}{\text{\# light piece C to cut}}$$

$$\frac{\rule{3cm}{0.4pt}}{\text{\# connecting squares needed}} \times 2 = \frac{\rule{2cm}{0.4pt}}{\text{\# dark piece C to cut}}$$

Sewing: Sew piece A to the end side of pattern piece B. The point of pattern piece A should match up exactly with the point of pattern piece B (Fig. 12–15). The right angle forms the corner of the unit and should be kept free.

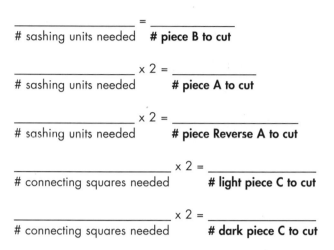

Fig. 12–15

On the other side of pattern piece B, sew pattern piece Reverse A. Match up the points again. See Figure 12–15. Repeat the same sewing sequence on the other end of the sashing strip to make a sashing unit (Fig. 12–16).

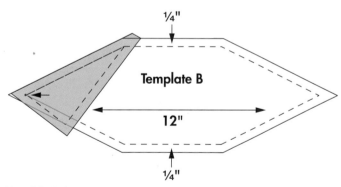

Fig. 12–16

Photo 47. Detail, STARS FOR LADY LIBERTY
    by Mary Ellen Von Holt and friends.
    54-40 or Fight sashing.

Sew a dark square (C) to a light square (C) (Fig. 12–17). Make two of these units and sew the two units together with a dark square touching a light square (Fig. 12–18) to make a Four-Patch connecting block.

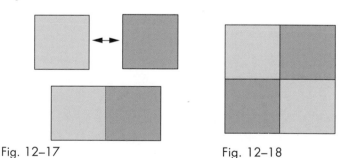

Fig. 12–17   Fig. 12–18

Alternate blocks with sashing units to make a row the desired width of the quilt top as shown in Figure 12–19.

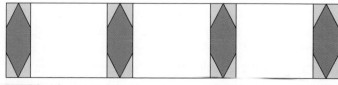

Fig. 12–19

Sew sashing units together with the Four-Patch connecting blocks to make strips the width needed for the quilt top (Fig. 12–20).

Fig. 12–20

Assemble the quilt top by sewing rows of blocks/sashing units to row with sashing units/connecting blocks (Fig. 12–21).

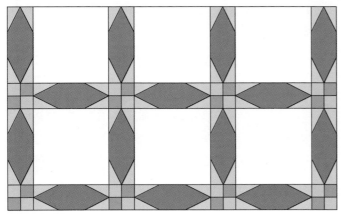

Fig. 12–21

PIECED SASHINGS

The variety of pieced sashings is unlimited. Pieced sashings can range from simple squares to triangles or diamonds. If the parts for a pieced sashing can be drafted with a pencil and paper, the parts can be sewn into numerous interesting sashings.

SQUARES

Using pieced squares to make a sashing strip can be as simple as using a single row of squares or using two or more rows of squares to make double, triple, etc. rows in each sashing strip (Photo 48).

Pattern: None

Worksheet: Squares sashing, page 105.

Sizing of Sashing: The size of the squares to be used for the sashing will be determined by dividing the finished width of the block into equal units and choosing either wide or narrow sashing. For example, an 8" block will divide equally into eight 1" squares for a narrow sashing or into four 2" squares for a wider sashing (Fig. 13–1).

Photo 48. GOOD TIMES
by the author. Squares sashing.

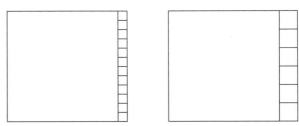

8" block with 1" squares   **8" block with 2" squares**

Fig. 13–1

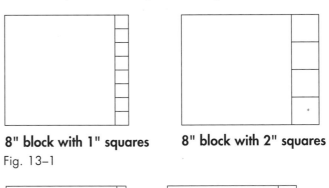

12" block with 1" squares   **12" block with 2" squares**

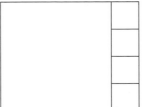

12" block with 3" squares

Fig. 13–2

For a 12" block, the divisions could be twelve 1" squares, six 2" squares, and four 3" squares (Fig. 13-2). The divisions on page 52 demonstrate the number of possible variations.

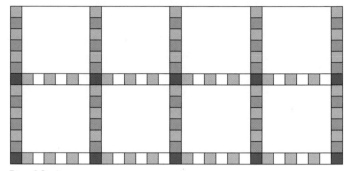

$$\frac{\rule{3cm}{0.4pt}}{\text{finished square size}} + \frac{1}{2}\text{" for seams} = \frac{\rule{3cm}{0.4pt}}{\textbf{size to cut squares}}$$

$$\frac{\rule{3cm}{0.4pt}}{\text{finished block width}} \div \frac{\rule{3cm}{0.4pt}}{\text{finished square size}} = \frac{\rule{3cm}{0.4pt}}{\substack{\textbf{\# squares for} \\ \textbf{sashing}}}$$

$$\frac{\rule{3cm}{0.4pt}}{\text{sashing unit squares}} \times \frac{\rule{3cm}{0.4pt}}{\text{\# sashing units}} = \frac{\rule{3cm}{0.4pt}}{\substack{\textbf{squares needed for} \\ \textbf{sashing units}}}$$

$$\frac{\rule{3cm}{0.4pt}}{\substack{\text{squares needed for} \\ \text{sashing units}}} + \frac{\rule{3cm}{0.4pt}}{\text{connecting squares}} = \frac{\rule{3cm}{0.4pt}}{\textbf{\#squares to cut}}$$

The connecting blocks for double or triple rows can be either the same size squares, solid blocks, or pieced blocks such as Quarter-Square Triangle blocks, stars, or any variety of Four-Patch or Nine-Patch blocks. Make a paper quilt (page 5) to explore the many possibilities.

Cutting: Cut the number of required squares as determined in the formula.

Sewing: Sew the squares together in rows that are the length of the block to make a sashing unit (Fig. 13–3).

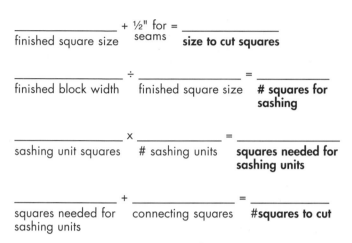

Fig. 13–3

Alternate blocks with sashing units to make rows the width of the quilt top (Fig. 13–4).

Fig. 13–4

Sew sashing units together with connecting squares to make rows the width of the quilt top (Fig. 13–5).

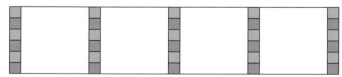

Fig. 13–5

Sets & Sashings for Quilts – Phyllis D. Miller

Assemble the quilt top by sewing block/sashing units to the rows of squares (Fig. 13–6).

Fig. 13–6

SQUARES ON POINT

Pattern: 3" wide sashing that can be used with 9", 12", 15", or 18" blocks, page 128.

Worksheet: Squares on Point sashing, page 106.

Sizing of Sashing: The number of pieces needed for each sashing unit for the Square on Point sashing is shown under the cutting instructions along with a diagram of the sashing unit.

Photo 49. FINALLY!!
by Carla Kilkelly. Squares on Point sashing.

The connecting blocks can be plain blocks or Squares on Point blocks. The directions use the Squares on Point blocks as the connecting blocks.

Determine the number of sashing units and connecting blocks needed by making a paper quilt as described on page 5. Find the number of each pattern piece that is needed for a sashing unit under the cutting instructions below.

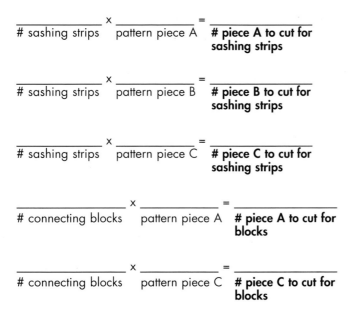

_____ x _____ = _____
sashing strips   pattern piece A   **# piece A to cut for sashing strips**

_____ x _____ = _____
sashing strips   pattern piece B   **# piece B to cut for sashing strips**

_____ x _____ = _____
sashing strips   pattern piece C   **# piece C to cut for sashing strips**

_____ x _____ = _____
connecting blocks   pattern piece A   **# piece A to cut for blocks**

_____ x _____ = _____
connecting blocks   pattern piece C   **# piece C to cut for blocks**

Cutting: For each sashing unit, cut the number of pieces for each pattern piece as indicated below.

For 9" block
- cut 3 pattern piece A
- cut 4 pattern piece B
- cut 4 pattern piece C

For 12" block
- cut 4 pattern piece A
- cut 6 pattern piece B
- cut 4 pattern piece C

For 15" block
- cut 5 pattern piece A
- cut 8 pattern piece B
- cut 4 pattern piece C

For 18" block
- cut 6 pattern piece A
- cut 10 pattern piece B
- cut 4 pattern piece C

For each connecting block
- cut 1 pattern piece A
- cut 4 pattern piece C

Sewing: Sew a piece C to two adjacent sides of piece A, and then sew piece A to a piece B (Fig. 13–7) to make one end unit of the sashing. Another end unit will be needed to finish opposite end of each sashing strip.

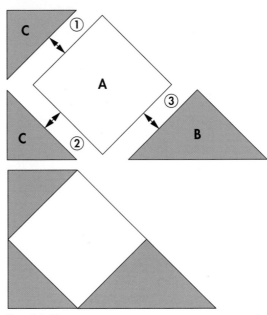

Fig. 13–7

Sew a piece B to a piece A and then sew this unit to a piece B (Fig. 13–8) to make a sashing unit.

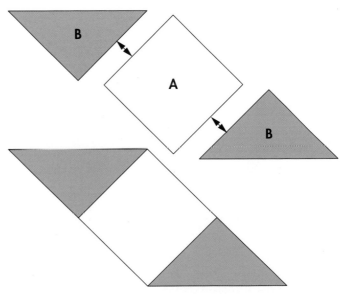

Fig. 13–8

Lay out the units as shown in Figure 13–9 and sew the units together, as indicated by the arrows, into a sashing strip.

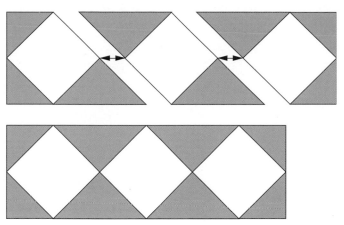

Fig. 13–9

The connecting blocks are made by sewing a piece C to each of the four sides of piece A (Fig. 13–10).

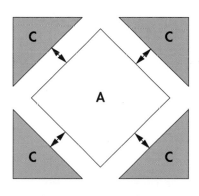

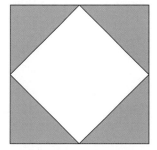

Fig. 13–10

Alternate blocks with sashing strips to make a row the desired width of the quilt top. Sew sashing units together with connecting blocks to make a row the width of the quilt top.

Sew a block/sashing strip row to a sashing unit/connecting block row to complete the quilt top (Fig. 13–11).

Fig. 13–11

DIAMONDS

Diamond sashings can be used effectively to emphasize a design in the blocks. Using templates for the pieces results in a more accurate Diamond sashing.

DARTING MINNOWS

This sashing is narrow at only 2" wide and is usually pieced with the diamonds and connecting blocks from a light fabric and the triangles from a darker fabric (Photo 50).

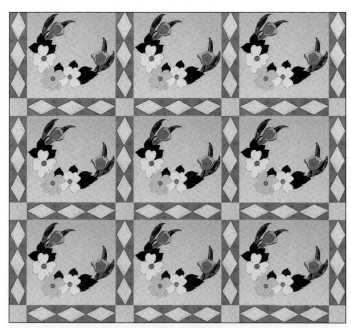

Photo 50. Detail, WELCOMING SPRING by the author. Darting Minnows sashing.

Pattern: 2" wide sashing for blocks divisible by 4, page 128.

Worksheet: Darting Minnows sashing, page 107.

Sizing of Sashing: Determine the number of sashing strips needed by making a paper quilt as described on page 5. The number of each pattern piece needed for a sashing unit for both 8" and 12" blocks is listed under the cutting instructions. The patterns can also be used with 16" or 20" blocks by adding more diamonds and triangles.

$$\underline{\hspace{3cm}} \times \underline{\hspace{3cm}} = \underline{\hspace{3cm}}$$
sashing units   pattern piece A   **# piece A to cut**

$$\underline{\hspace{3cm}} \times \underline{\hspace{3cm}} = \underline{\hspace{3cm}}$$
sashing units   pattern piece B   **# piece B to cut**

$$\underline{\hspace{3cm}} \times \underline{\hspace{3cm}} = \underline{\hspace{3cm}}$$
sashing units   pattern piece C   **# piece C to cut**

$$\underline{\hspace{3cm}} \times \underline{\hspace{3cm}} = \underline{\hspace{3cm}}$$
sashing units   pattern piece Rev. C   **# piece Rev. C to cut**

$$\underline{\hspace{3cm}} = \underline{\hspace{3cm}}$$
connecting blocks needed   **# 2½" squares to cut**

Cutting: The following chart gives the number of pieces needed for each sashing unit for both the 8" and 12" blocks. Use these numbers in the above formulas for the pattern piece to determine the total number of each pattern piece needed.

For 8" block
- cut 2 pattern piece A
- cut 2 pattern piece B
- cut 2 pattern piece C
- cut 2 pattern piece Reverse C

For 12" block
- cut 3 pattern piece A
- cut 4 pattern piece B
- cut 2 pattern piece C
- cut 2 pattern piece Reverse C

Don't forget to cut the 2½" squares for the connecting blocks.

Sewing: The easiest method of construction is to sew the pieces together into units and then into the sashing strip. The sewing instructions are for the 12" block. Eliminate one of the units for an 8" block.

Sew a Reverse C piece to piece A and sew this unit to a piece B (Fig. 13–12).

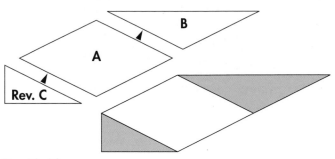

Fig. 13–12

Next, sew a piece B to a piece A and sew this unit to another piece B (Fig. 13–13).

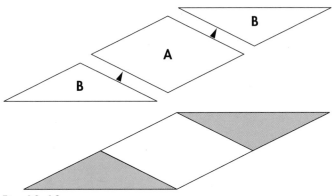

Fig. 13–13

Lay out the units as shown in Figure 13–14 and sew them together to make a sashing unit; sew a C piece and a Reverse C to complete each end of the unit.

Fig. 13–14

Alternate blocks with sashing units to make a row the width of the quilt top (Fig. 13–15).

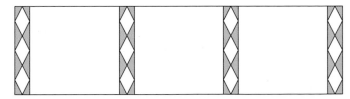

Fig. 13–15

Sew sashing units together using connecting blocks to make a row that goes across the width of the quilt top (Fig. 13–16).

Fig. 13–16

Sew a block/sashing unit row to a sashing unit/connecting block row. Continue sewing rows to rows to finish constructing the quilt top (Fig. 13–17).

Fig. 13–17

DIAMOND ROW

This sashing is composed of a row of diamonds that are standing on point and are connected with triangles to form a sashing row (Photo 51).

Pattern: The pattern on page 129 for the Diamond Row sashing is 4" wide and can be used with any block that is divisible by 2 such as 8", 10", 12", or 14" blocks.

Worksheet: Diamond Row sashing, page 108.

Sizing of Sashing: Determine the number of sashing units needed by making a paper quilt as described on page 5. The number of pieces needed for each sashing unit for a 12" block is listed under the cutting instructions.

_____ x _____ = _____
\# sashing units   pattern piece A   **# piece A to cut**

_____ x _____ = _____
\# sashing units   pattern piece B   **# piece B to cut**

Photo 51. Detail, POT OF PRIMROSES
by Lou Ann Philpot. Diamond Row sashing.

_____ x _____ = _____
\# sashing units   pattern piece C   **# piece C to cut**

_____ x _____ = _____
\# sashing units   pattern piece Reverse C   **# piece Reverse C to cut**

_____ = _____
\# connecting blocks needed   **# 4½" squares to cut**

Cutting: For a 12" block, cut the following number of pieces for each sashing unit. To make the sashing fit a smaller block, take away one diamond unit to decrease the size by 2" or, for a larger block, add a diamond unit to increase the sashing by 2". Use these numbers in the above formulas to determine the total number of each pattern piece to cut.

For a 12" block
- cut 6 pattern piece A
- cut 10 pattern piece B
- cut 2 pattern piece C
- cut 2 pattern piece Reverse C

Plus, cut the number of required 4½" squares for the connecting blocks.

Sewing: The easiest method of construction is to sew the pieces together in diagonal units and then sew those units together. Make the first diagonal row by sewing piece Reverse C to a piece A. Sew this unit to a piece B (Fig. 13–18).

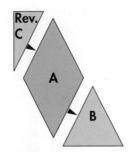
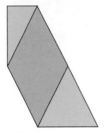

Fig. 13–18

For the next unit, the sewing sequence will be a piece B sewn to piece A, sew this unit to another piece B (Fig. 13–19).

The diagonal units can now be assembled as shown in Figure 13–20; sew a piece C or a reverse C to each end to complete the sashing unit.

Alternate a sashing unit with a connecting block to make a sashing strip the width needed for the quilt top. Refer to the paper quilt for the numbers.

Sew a sashing unit to the sides of the quilt blocks to make a sashing/block row the width needed.

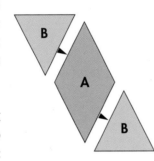
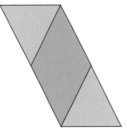

Fig. 13–19

When the rows are complete, sew a sashing strip row to a sashing/block to complete the quilt top (Fig. 13–21).

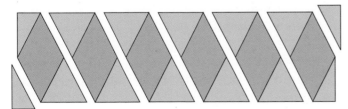

Fig. 13–20

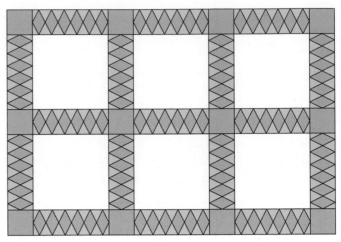

Fig. 13–21

BRAIDED

The Braided sashing is created by alternating light and dark diamonds to form a braided look with solid squares for connecting blocks. Braided sashing can be done in two colors, one light and one dark, or it can be made with a variety of light and dark fabrics and colors for a scrappy look (Photo 52).

Pattern: The Braided sashing pattern is on page 130. The pattern shown makes a sashing that is 2¾" wide and will fit any block that is divisible by 4, such as an 8", 12", or 16" block.

Worksheet: Braided sashing, page 109.

Sizing of Sashing: Make a paper quilt by following the instructions on page 5 to determine the number of sashing units required. Read and look at all of the illustrations before counting. The number of pieces needed of each pattern piece for one sashing unit for an 8" block is shown under the cutting instructions. Each diamond piece is equal to 2" in the sashing and the length can be changed by using more or fewer diamonds.

$$\underline{\hspace{3cm}} \times \underline{\hspace{3cm}} = \underline{\hspace{3cm}}$$
sashing Unit 1   pattern piece A   **# piece A to cut**

$$\underline{\hspace{3cm}} \times \underline{\hspace{3cm}} = \underline{\hspace{3cm}}$$
sashing Unit 2   pattern piece A   **# piece Reverse A to cut**

$$\underline{\hspace{2cm}} \times 2 = \underline{\hspace{3cm}}$$
blocks   **# piece B to cut**

# Unit 1 around quilt edge	=	# **dark piece C to cut**
# Unit 2 around quilt edge	=	# **light piece C to cut**
# Unit 1 around quilt edge	=	# **light piece D to cut**
# Unit 2 around quilt edge	=	# **light piece Reverse D to cut**

Cutting: The totals for each pattern piece are provided in the cutting chart. This makes the sashing units for a 8" block. Note that there are light and dark fabrics for pattern pieces A and C. Use the numbers in the formulas and cut that number of lights and darks for each pattern piece.

- cut pattern piece A
  2 light and 2 dark
- cut pattern piece Reverse A
  2 light and 2 dark
- cut pattern piece B
  2 light
- cut pattern piece C
  4 light and 4 dark for the corners
- cut pattern piece C
  1 light for each Unit 2 around quilt edge
- cut pattern piece C
  1 dark for each Unit 1 around quilt edge
- cut pattern piece D
  1 light for each Unit 1 around quilt edge
- cut pattern piece Reverse D
  1 light for each Unit 2 around quilt edge

Sewing: The diamonds will need to be sewn to make two different units. Begin with Unit 1 by sewing a light Piece A diamond to a piece A dark diamond. Alternate light and dark until the strip contains 4 diamonds (Fig. 13–22). You will need two of Unit 1 for each block plus the number needed for the outside edges of the quilt top.

Unit 1

Fig. 13–22

Photo 52. Detail, KENTUCKY ROSE WREATH by the author. Braided sashing.

Unit 2 sashing strip is sewn in the same way except this time the light/dark sequence is reversed. Start with a Reverse A dark diamond, then a Reverse A light diamond, etc. (Fig. 13–23). You will need two of Unit 2 for each block plus enough for the outside edges of the quilt top.

Unit 2

Fig. 13–23

Every other block in the quilt top will have a Unit 1 sashing at the top and bottom of the block and the rest of the blocks will have Unit 2 sashings at the top and bottom. If the blocks have a definite "up," lay out the blocks before sewing. Blocks that look the same when turned can be rotated, and therefore can have the sashing units all sewn the same.

Sew a sashing Unit 1 to the top and bottom of the block as shown in Figure 13–24; one starts with a light diamond, the next with a dark diamond. Be sure to sew only on the sewing lines. Do not sew through the seam allowances so the diamonds can be sewn in when the other sashing strips are sewn to the block.

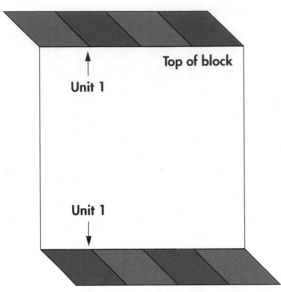

Fig. 13–24

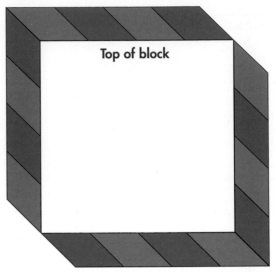

Fig. 13–26

Next, sew a sashing Unit 2 to each side of the block (Fig. 13–25). Your blocks should now look like Figure 13–26.

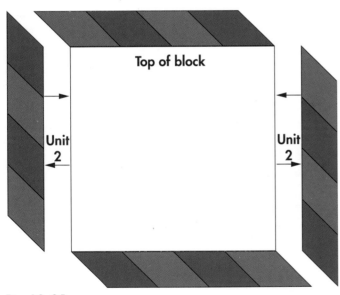

Fig. 13–25

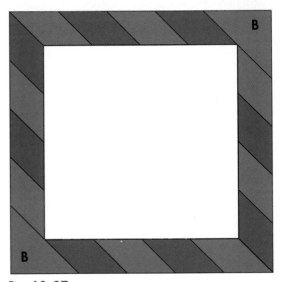

Fig. 13–27

Sew a piece B to the two opposite corners of the block (Fig. 13–27). A triangle (B) will be at the right top.

Follow the same sewing sequence for blocks that have a definite top by sewing Unit 2 strips to the top and the bottom of the block. These blocks should look like the one in Figure 13–28. A triangle (B) will be at the left top.

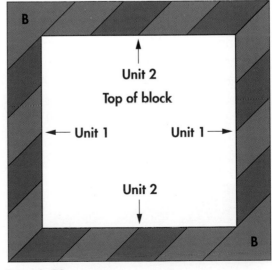

Fig. 13–28

To assemble the quilt top, sew the blocks together in rows starting with a right top triangle block and sew it to a left top triangle block (Fig. 13–29). Continue alternating block units until the desired width is attained. The second row will start with a left top triangle block, next with a right top triangle block, etc. (Fig. 13–30).

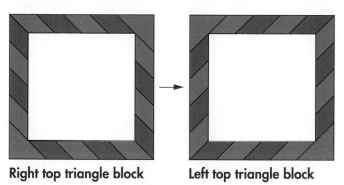

Right top triangle block   **Left top triangle block**

Fig. 13–29

Row 1

Row 2

Fig. 13–30

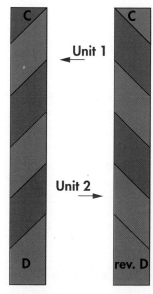

Fig. 13–31

When the rows are complete, a sashing unit must be added to each end of the rows to make the braid. The top and the bottom of the quilt top will also need sashing units added to complete the braid. Sew a piece D to the dark diamond end and dark piece C to the light diamond end of a Unit 1. Sew a Reverse D piece to the light diamond end and a light piece C to the dark diamond end of a Unit 2 (Fig. 13–31). Sew one of these new units to the ends of the block rows by matching a Unit 1 piece to a Unit 2 (Fig. 13–32). Be careful in matching the diamond points when sewing the two units together.

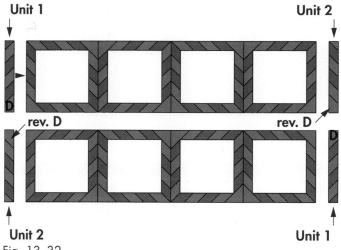

Fig. 13–32

Sew a light piece C and a dark piece C together, across the diagonal, to make a Half-Square Triangle block. Make two of these blocks, one for each end of the row.

Sew a row of the new units (Fig. 13–31) to go across the quilt top by beginning with a Half-Square Triangle block, alternating units, and being sure that a Unit 1 will be above a Unit 2 block, and ending with a Half-Square Triangle block (Fig. 13–33).

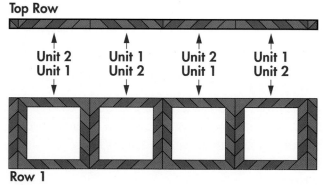

Fig. 13–33

To construct the quilt top, sew the sashing units row to the first block row. Sew Row 1 to Row 2 and continue until all of the rows are sewn together (Fig. 13–34). Add another sashing units row to the quilt bottom to finish the quilt (Fig. 13–35).

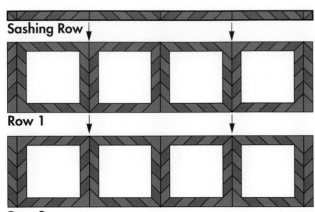

Sashing Row

Row 1

Row 2

Fig. 13–34

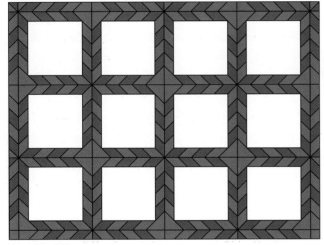

Fig. 13–35

TRIANGLES

Many types of triangles can be used for sashing strips. The triangles can be right angles, or they can be short and fat, or long and thin. You might want to choose a triangle from the block to repeat in the sashing.

SAWTOOTH

Simple half-square triangles are used to make the Sawtooth sashing. It can be made in two colors or a variety of colors and fabrics (Photo 53).

Pattern: None

Worksheet: Sawtooth sashing, page 110.

Sizing of Sashing: The size of the sashing can vary from 1" wide to 3" wide, and perhaps for very large blocks, it could be as wide as 4" . This sashing is most pleasing when the sawteeth are fairly small. Blocks that measure 12" of larger would look best

with a 2" wide Sawtooth sashing. Smaller blocks should have either 1" or 1½" wide sashing.

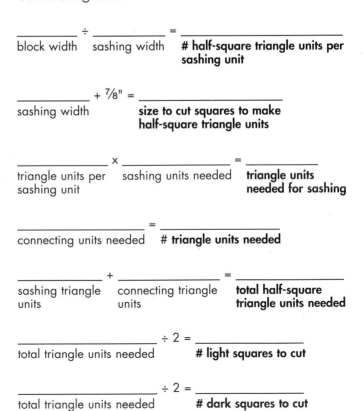

Photo 53. LITTLE BROWN BIRD by Margaret Docherty. Sawtooth sashing.

Make a paper quilt (see page 5) to determine the number of sashing units needed and the number of connecting units.

$$\frac{}{\text{block width}} \div \frac{}{\text{sashing width}} = \frac{}{\substack{\text{\# half-square triangle units per} \\ \text{sashing unit}}}$$

$$\frac{}{\text{sashing width}} + \tfrac{7}{8}" = \frac{}{\substack{\text{size to cut squares to make} \\ \text{half-square triangle units}}}$$

$$\frac{}{\substack{\text{triangle units per} \\ \text{sashing unit}}} \times \frac{}{\text{sashing units needed}} = \frac{}{\substack{\text{triangle units} \\ \text{needed for sashing}}}$$

$$\frac{}{\text{connecting units needed}} = \frac{}{\text{\# triangle units needed}}$$

$$\frac{}{\substack{\text{sashing triangle} \\ \text{units}}} + \frac{}{\substack{\text{connecting triangle} \\ \text{units}}} = \frac{}{\substack{\text{total half-square} \\ \text{triangle units needed}}}$$

$$\frac{}{\text{total triangle units needed}} \div 2 = \frac{}{\text{\# light squares to cut}}$$

$$\frac{}{\text{total triangle units needed}} \div 2 = \frac{}{\text{\# dark squares to cut}}$$

Fig. 14–1

Cutting: Cut the total number of squares needed from light and dark fabric. Use quick rotary cutting methods.

Sewing: On the wrong side of the light fabric square, use a ruler and a fabric marking pencil or pen to mark a diagonal line from the upper corner to the lower corner (Photo 54).

Photo 54.

Place the marked light fabric square with the right side facing the right side of the dark fabric square. Sew a seam ¼" in from the marked line on both sides of the marked line (Photo 55). Mark a sewing line, if needed. Cut between the two seams on the marked line using either a rotary cutter or scissors. Open and press the seam allowance toward the dark fabric. You

Photo 55.

Photo 56.

should have a half-square triangle unit as shown in Photo 56. Trim off the fabric tips that stick out beyond the edges of the square.

Sew the half-square triangle units together to make sashing units the width of the block. All of the dark triangles should be at the bottom and the light triangles at the top (Fig. 14–1).

Make a sashing row the width of the quilt top by sewing the sashing units with the half-square triangle connecting blocks. You should have a complete row of half-square triangles the width of the quilt top with the dark triangles at the bottom of the row.

Sew half-square triangle sashing units to the sides of the blocks to make a row the width of the quilt top. Sew the triangle units to the blocks so that the dark side of the blocks is the same between all the blocks (Fig. 14–2).

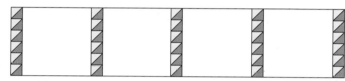

Fig. 14–2

Assemble the quilt top by sewing a row of half-square triangle blocks to a sashing/block row, then a row of triangle blocks, sashing/block row, etc. until the quilt top is the desired size (Fig. 14–3).

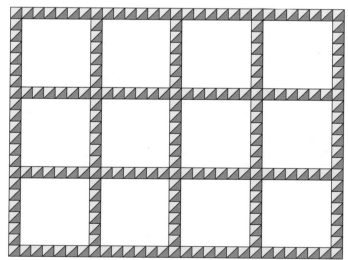

Fig. 14–3

FLYING GEESE

This sashing consists of triangles that represent "geese flying" in one direction. It can be used with regular square blocks with a choice of connecting squares or is a good choice for a Bars set. When the Flying Geese sashing is used with blocks, the connecting block can be a pieced block or a plain fabric block (Photo 57).

Photo 57. Detail, FLYING IN ALL DIRECTIONS by the author. Flying Geese sashing.

Pattern: 4" wide sashing, Flying Geese pattern with Square on Point connecting block pattern, page 131.

Worksheet: Flying Geese Sashing, page 111.

Sizing of Sashing: The pattern for the Flying Geese sashing will make a sashing that is 4" wide and will work with any block that is divisible by 2. For example, a 12" block would require six Flying Geese units.

Make a paper quilt following the instructions on page 5 to determine the number of sashing units required to make the quilt top.

$$\frac{}{\text{quilt block width}} \div 2 = \frac{}{\text{\# geese units needed for sashing unit}}$$

$$\frac{}{\substack{\text{geese units for}\\\text{one sashing}}} \times \frac{}{\text{\# sashing units needed}} = \frac{}{\text{total geese units}}$$

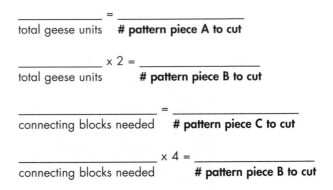

$$\frac{}{\text{total geese units}} = \frac{}{\text{\# pattern piece A to cut}}$$

$$\frac{}{\text{total geese units}} \times 2 = \frac{}{\text{\# pattern piece B to cut}}$$

$$\frac{}{\text{connecting blocks needed}} = \frac{}{\text{\# pattern piece C to cut}}$$

$$\frac{}{\text{connecting blocks needed}} \times 4 = \frac{}{\text{\# pattern piece B to cut}}$$

Cutting: Pattern piece A has the grain line along the long edge or base of the triangle. Be sure to remember this when cutting.

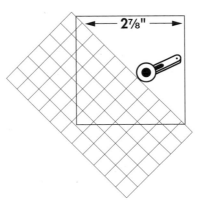

Fig. 14–4

Pattern piece B can be rotary cut by cutting the fabric in 2⅞" squares and then cutting the squares diagonally in half from corner to corner (Fig. 14–4). Each square will make two half-square triangles or two pattern B pieces.

Each connecting block will require two 2⅞" squares to make four pattern piece B triangles.

Sewing: Lay Piece A down with the base of the triangle toward you and the right side of the fabric up. With the right side of the fabric up, lay piece B to the left and a rotated piece B to the right (Fig. 14–5).

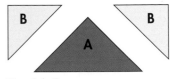

Fig. 14–5

Match up the points on the lower left of both triangles (A and B); sew this seam. Press to make a unit as shown in Fig. 14–6). Match up the points on the lower right of both triangles (A and rotated B); sew this seam. Press to make a completed "geese" unit (Fig. 14–7).

Fig. 14–6

Fig. 14–7

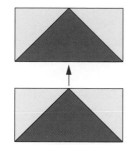

Fig. 14–8

The geese units are sewn with the point of A triangles going in the same direction (Fig. 14–8). Sew the number of geese units together that are needed for a sashing unit or a Bars sashing strip.

To make the Square on Point connecting block (Fig. 14–9), sew a B triangle to one side of the C square (Fig. 14–10). Match up the seam lines where the corner of the square and the point of the triangle connect. Continue sewing triangles to the other three sides of the square. Press.

Fig. 14–9

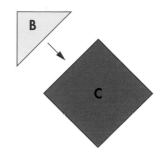

Fig. 14–10

To assemble the quilt top, decide which direction the geese will fly. This can be done on the paper quilt or by actually placing the sashing units and the blocks out on a bed or design wall.

If using the Bars set, refer to the sewing instructions for the Bars set on page 15 to make a quilt top as shown in Figure 14–11.

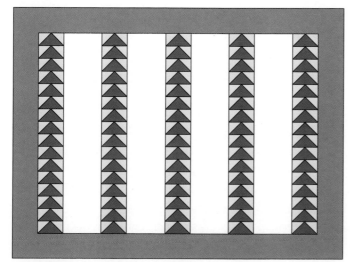

Fig. 14–11

For the Straight set, sew the sashing units and blocks together to make rows. The Flying Geese sashing units can fly alternately up and down. Make a row the width of the quilt top by sewing sashing units and connecting blocks (Fig. 14–12). The geese alternate directions in this row also.

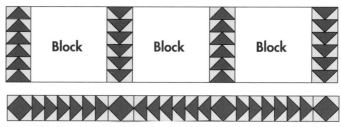

Fig. 14–12

Sew the block/sashing units rows to the sashing unit/connecting block row to finish the quilt top.

SHOOTING STARS

This complex appearing sashing is actually just two elongated triangles. When sewn with light and dark fabrics a secondary four-pointed star appears. This sashing should be planned by using the worksheet quilt on page 112 to determine the light/dark placement. Place a sheet of tracing paper over the worksheet quilt and color or shade in the design. The worksheet quilt can be enlarged to make it easier to color and more blocks and sashing rows can be added if needed. In Doreen Perkins' PRESIDENTIAL BLUES quilt, one color family is used in a variety of fabrics that are light, medium, dark, and bright (Photo 58).

Photo 58. Detail, PRESIDENTIAL BLUES by Doreen Perkins. Shooting Stars sashing.

Pattern: Pattern on page 132 makes a 2" wide sashing for an 8" block.

Worksheet: Shooting Stars sashing, page 112.

Sizing of Sashing: If the block being used is larger than 8", draft a new pattern by drawing a rectangle the length of the block. Increase the width of the sashing by ½" increments until it looks pleasing. The longer the sashing unit, the wider the sashing strip will need to be.

$$\frac{\text{_____}}{\text{\# sashing units needed}} = \frac{\text{_____}}{\text{\# piece A to cut}}$$

$$\frac{\text{_____}}{\text{\# sashing units needed}} = \frac{\text{_____}}{\text{\# piece B to cut}}$$

$$\frac{\text{_____}}{\text{\# connecting blocks needed}} = \frac{\text{_____}}{\text{\# 2½" squares to cut}}$$

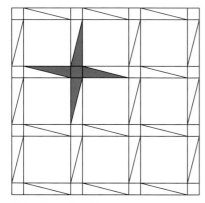

One Star Set Cut

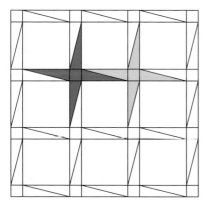

Second Star Set Cut
Fig. 14–13

Cutting: For each star of one color/fabric, cut two A pieces, two B pieces and one connecting block. Cut one star set and place it with the quilt blocks on a design wall. Next, cut the star set that will touch the previous star (Fig. 14–13). This helps decide if the next star needs to be light or dark or bright. It is preferable to cut all of the sashing pieces before sewing to see if you like the way the quilt looks.

Sewing: To sew a sashing unit, place an A piece right side facing a B piece. Pin at the points and along the seam line to be sure that the point of the

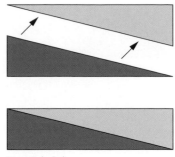

star will stay sharp when sewn (Fig. 14–14). Press the seam allowances toward the darker fabric. Return the finished sashing unit to its proper place on the design wall. Sew all of the sashing units in the same way.

Fig. 14–14

When all of the sashing units have been sewn, sew a sashing unit to a connecting block, another sashing unit, etc., until a row the width of the quilt top is finished. Sew a row of sashing units and blocks to make row the width of the quilt top (Fig. 14–15).

Sashing Unit/Connector Block Row

Sashing Unit/Block Row
Fig. 14–15

Finish the quilt top by sewing the sashing/connecting block rows to the sashing/block rows (Fig. 14–16).

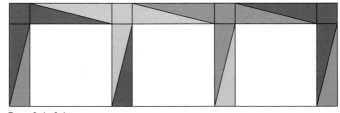

Fig. 14–16

NEW YORK BEAUTY

This sashing with its long, sharp triangles is an exciting addition to the traditional block of the same name. It also will work well with Mariner's Compass or large appliqué blocks. The sashing pattern has a connecting block designed by the author. This connecting block could be replaced with a 6" Eight-pointed Star or Compass block (Photo 59).

Pattern: 6" wide sashing, connecting block, page 133.

Worksheet: New York Beauty sashing, page 113.

Sizing of Sashing: The total number of pieces, listed under the cutting directions, is for an 18" block. The sashing is 6" wide with a 6" square connecting block. Each triangle (pattern piece A) is 1", making it easy to increase or decrease the length of the sashing.

Make a paper quilt (page 5) to determine the number of sashing units and connecting blocks needed.

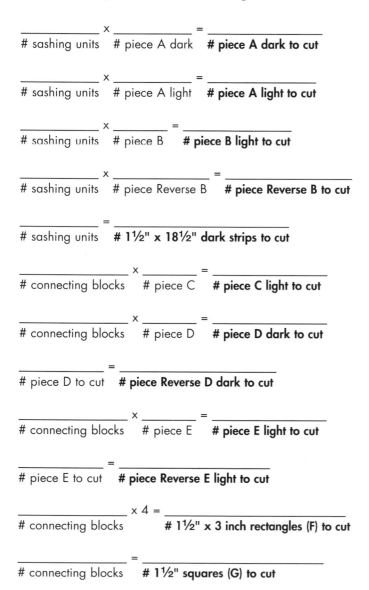

_____ x _____ = _____
\# sashing units \# piece A dark **\# piece A dark to cut**

_____ x _____ = _____
\# sashing units \# piece A light **\# piece A light to cut**

_____ x _____ = _____
\# sashing units \# piece B **\# piece B light to cut**

_____ x _____ = _____
\# sashing units \# piece Reverse B **\# piece Reverse B to cut**

_____ = _____
\# sashing units **\# 1½" x 18½" dark strips to cut**

_____ x _____ = _____
\# connecting blocks \# piece C **\# piece C light to cut**

_____ x _____ = _____
\# connecting blocks \# piece D **\# piece D dark to cut**

_____ = _____
\# piece D to cut **\# piece Reverse D dark to cut**

_____ x _____ = _____
\# connecting blocks \# piece E **\# piece E light to cut**

_____ = _____
\# piece E to cut **\# piece Reverse E light to cut**

_____ x 4 = _____
\# connecting blocks **\# 1½" x 3 inch rectangles (F) to cut**

_____ = _____
\# connecting blocks **\# 1½" squares (G) to cut**

Photo 59. Detail, NEBRASKA BEAUTY by Joan L. Schwalm. New York Beauty sashing.

Cutting: All of the pieces for the New York Beauty sashing should be cut by making templates, marking around the template, and then cutting. The squares and rectangles can be rotary cut. Be sure to make small holes in the templates as shown on the patterns (page 133) and mark these dots on the fabric pieces for accuracy in piecing.

For each 18" long sashing unit, cut:
- cut pattern piece A – 36 dark
- cut pattern piece A – 32 light
- cut pattern piece B – 2 light
- cut pattern piece Reverse B – 2 light

For each connecting block, cut:
- cut pattern piece C – 4 light
- cut pattern piece D – 4 dark
- cut pattern piece Reverse D – 4 dark
- cut pattern piece E – 4 light
- cut pattern piece Reverse E – 4 light
- cut pattern piece F – 4 dark
- cut pattern piece G – 1 light

Sewing: Pin the pieces right sides together being careful to match the dots at the points. Sew a light piece A to a dark A to make 18 sections (Fig. 14–17). Sew these sections together by carefully matching the points (Fig. 14–18). Continue sewing sections together until there are 18 dark A pieces on one side. Add a light B at one end and a Reverse light B at the other end to finish the strip (Fig. 14–19). The sashing unit has two of these strips, so repeat the sewing sequence to make a second strip.

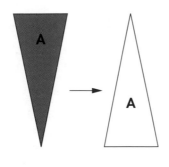

Fig. 14–17

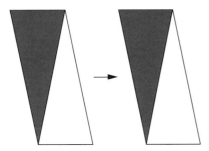

Fig. 14–18

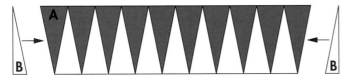

Fig. 14–19

Sew a plain dark strip to the light sides of the pieced strips (Fig. 14–20). Press the seams to the center.

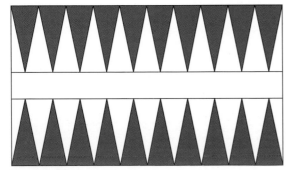

Fig. 14–20

To make the connecting block (Fig. 14–21), four corner sections need to be pieced. Lay out the pieces as shown in Figure 14–22. Pin the pieces at the points and sew the pieces together as indicated by the arrows. Make 4 identical sections. Lay out the block as shown in Figure 14–23 being sure that the large corner of piece C is pointing to the center. Sew each row of the block. Stitch the rows together to complete the block.

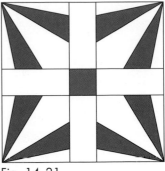

Fig. 14–21

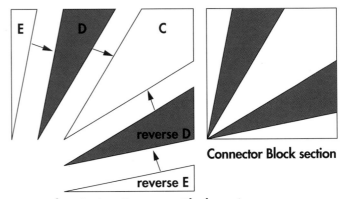

Connector Block section

Layout for piecing Connector Block section
Fig. 14–22

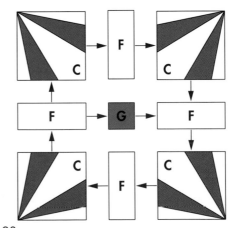

Fig. 14–23

Sew sashing units and connecting blocks together to make a sashing row the desired length.

Sew sashing units to the sides of the blocks to make a row the desired length or quilt width.

To complete the quilt top, refer to the assembly directions in the Sets section for the set you have chosen.

RECTANGLES

Rectangles can be joined together by abutting them or sewing them in diagonal rows to create visually pleasing sashing strips.

TWIST AND TURN

Several variations can be achieved by changing color placement or light, medium and dark placement. This sashing can be made from only two fabrics, three fabrics, or an assortment of colors and fabrics in lights, mediums, and darks. It is to be used in a Bars set and can be either the focal point of the quilt with plain strips between or can be used as sashing with the blocks set in bars (Photo 60).

Pattern: None

Worksheet: Twist and Turn sashing, page 114.

Sizing of Sashing: The directions given here will make a Bars set sashing that is 5 inches wide.

It is made of rectangles and, even though there is some waste of fabric, the sewing will be much easier than using templates or patterns.

_____ ÷ 2.75 = _____ x 2 = _____
sashing bar length   **total # rectangles**
                                            needed for one bar

_____ x _____ = _____
total bars needed   total rectangles for one bar   **# rectangles**
                                                    to cut

For two colors:

_____ ÷ 2 = _____
total # rectangles   **# to cut light rectangles**
                          and dark rectangles

For three colors or light, medium, dark values:

_____ ÷ 3 = _____
total # rectangles   **# to cut of each color or shade**

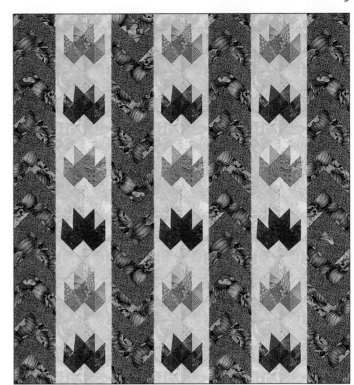

Photo 60. Detail, MAPLE LEAVES
by the author. Twist and Turn sashing.

Cutting: Cut rectangles that measure 2½" X 5½". Cut the number needed for each color or shade. Keep the rectangles separated in stacks of color or value.

Fig. 15–1

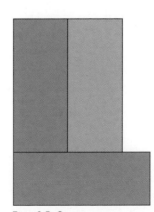

Fig. 15–2

Sewing: Sew a dark rectangle to a light rectangle (Fig. 15–1). Press the seam allowance toward the dark fabric. Sew a dark rectangle to the bottom of this unit (Fig. 15–2). Sew a light rectangle to the left side of this unit (Fig. 15–3, page 70). Next, sew another light rectangle to the bottom of this unit (Fig. 15–4, page 70). Continue sewing in the same sequence until the bar is the desired length. The strip will have uneven edges. Add extra color to this sashing by using three different colors (Fig. 15-5, page 70).

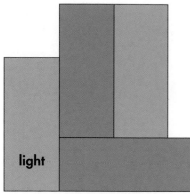

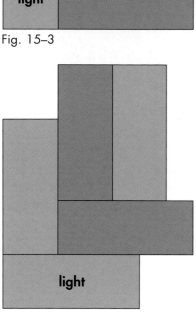

Fig. 15–3

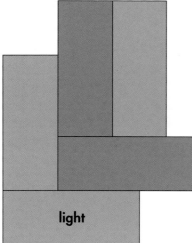

Fig. 15–4

When the strip or bar is sewn, use a long ruler to cut a straight edge on one side of the bar. The ruler edge should touch the upper end of the top rectangle and the corner seam lines (Fig. 15–6). Using the long ruler and a rotary cutter, make the same cut on the other side to create the sashing strip 5½" wide. Square off the ends of the sashing strips (Fig. 15–7). The sashing strip edges are bias so use care when handling and sewing.

Follow the instructions in the Bars set, page 14, to complete the quilt top.

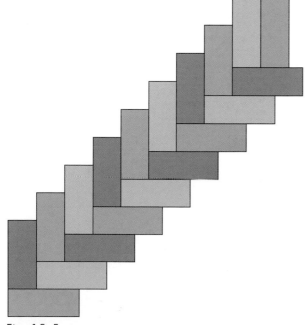

Fig. 15–5

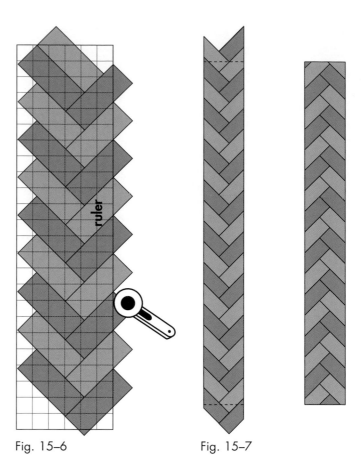

Fig. 15–6   Fig. 15–7

ROMAN STRIPE

This pieced sashing consists of narrow rectangles or bands of assorted fabrics. The width of the bands can be the same or varied. It is most successful in scraps, but could also be pieced in bands shaded from light to dark, or use two colors to give the appearance of stripes. This sashing can be used between blocks or as sashing strips in a Bars set (Photo 61).

Make a paper quilt, page 5, to determine the number of sashing units needed. The sashing strips can be set together with plain connecting blocks or Quarter-Square Triangle blocks (See page 37).

Pattern: None

Worksheet: Roman Stripe sashing, page 115.

Sizing of Sashing: The length of the sashing unit will be determined by the size of the block. The width of the rectangles or bands in the sashing unit can vary from ½" to 1". Use the 1" width for larger blocks. Determine the width of the sashing by the size of the quilt block or choose what is pleasing.

For this example, the sashing width will be 3" with ½" bands.

_____ + ½" for seams = _____
band width   **width to cut bands**

_____ + ½" for seams = _____
sashing width   **length to cut bands**

_____ ÷ _____ = _____
finished block width   finished band width   **# bands for each sashing unit**

_____ x _____ = _____
sashing units   # bands for each   **total bands to cut**
            sashing unit

_____ = _____
connecting blocks needed   **# 3½" squares to cut**

Cutting: The rectangles or bands can be rotary cut.

Sewing: With right sides together, sew two bands or rectangles together. Add another band to this unit and continue sewing bands to the strip until the required length of the sashing unit is obtained (Fig. 15–8). If bands of varied widths are used, the sew-and-flip paper foundation method is recommended.

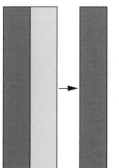

Sew sashing units and blocks together to make rows the width of the quilt top (Fig. 15–9).

Sew connecting blocks and sashing units together to make rows the width of the quilt top (Fig. 15–10).

Fig. 15–8

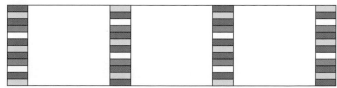

Fig. 15–9

Fig. 15–10

Photo 61. Detail, TOO MANY SUES by the author. Roman Stripe sashing.

Complete the quilt top assembly by following the directions in the Sets section for the set you have chosen.

DIAGONAL STRING

Make this sashing by sewing on a paper foundation. Use scraps of many fabrics and colors in strips of uneven strings. This is a good way to use leftovers from other projects. Use sashing with blocks or in the Bars set (Photo 62).

Photo 62. Detail, STRING STARS by the author. Diagonal String sashing.

Pattern: None

Worksheet: Diagonal String sashing, page 116.

Sizing of Sashing: Choose a width for the sashing by taking the size of the block into consideration. The larger the block, the wider the sashing can be. The length of the sashing unit will be determined by the block size. This sashing can be used with plain or pieced connecting blocks.

_____ + ½" = _____
sashing width   **finished width to make sashing unit**

_____ + ½" = _____
block width   **finished length to make sashing unit**

_____ + ½" = _____
sashing width   **size squares to cut for connecting blocks**

Cutting: Cut a paper foundation for each sashing unit needed. The paper should measure the same as the finished width and length above. The paper foundations include seam allowances.

Cut fabric scraps into strings that are either straight, or wedge-shaped or both. Cut the strings all the same width if an equal striped look is desired. The length of the strings should be approximately double the finished width needed to make the sashing.

If connecting blocks are used, cut squares the width of the sashing.

Photo 63.

Sewing: Start at one end of the foundation paper and place a fabric string diagonally across the width of the paper foundation with the right side up. Lay another string on top with right sides of the fabric together and one side of the fabric edges matching. Sew a ¼" seam along the matching edges (Photo 63). Press the top fabric away from the bottom fabric (Photo 64).

Add another fabric string with the right sides facing and the edges offset and sew this string (Photo 65). Trim excess fabric. Continue adding strings above and below to fill the paper foundation (Photo 66). Cut along the paper edge to trim off the excess ends of the strings. Remove the paper foundation and the sashing unit is complete. (Photo 67).

Photo 64.

Photo 65.

Sew sashing units and blocks together to make rows the width of the quilt top (Fig. 15–11).

Sew connecting blocks and sashing units together to make rows the desired width (Fig. 15–12).

Photo 66.

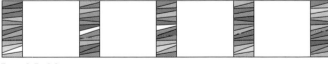
Photo 67.

Fig. 15–11

Fig. 15–12

To complete the quilt top, follow the directions in the Sets section for the set that you have chosen.

WEDDING RING TILE

The beauty of this design is that the sashing makes the quilt when used with plain octagonal blocks. It is also an effective sashing with octagonal shaped appliquéd blocks (Photo 68).

Pattern: Wedding Ring Tile block and sashing unit, pages 134 and 135.

Worksheet: Wedding Ring Tile sashing, page 117.

Sizing of Sashing: Refer to the directions in the Sets section for an Octagonal set and the paper quilt directions about determining the number of octagon units needed for the size quilt desired. Each Wedding Ring Tile block (Fig. 15–13) is 11¼" wide and long. The number of pieces for each pattern piece is listed under the cutting directions.

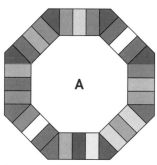
Fig. 15–13

_____	= _____
total # blocks	**# piece A to cut**

_____	x	_____	=	_____
total # blocks		# piece B needed		**total # piece B to cut**

_____	x	_____	=	_____
total # blocks		# piece C needed		**total # piece C to cut**

_____	= _____
total # setting squares needed	**# piece D to cut**

_____	= _____
total # side triangles needed	**# piece E to cut**

Cutting: For each octagonal Wedding Ring Tile unit:

- cut pattern piece A
    1 solid or background fabric
- cut pattern piece B
    24 from a variety of fabrics and colors
- cut pattern piece C
    8 from the same fabric or same color/shade
- cut pattern piece F
    4 solid or background fabric

Photo 68. A MAGICAL MARRIAGE
by the author. Wedding Ring Tile sashing.

Cut the squares (D) and triangles (E) and (F) from the solid or background fabric. Pattern piece B can be rotary cut. The measurement for pattern piece B is a rectangle 1½" X 2½".

Sewing: This pattern must fit exactly so check to be sure that your seams are exactly ¼" as shown on the pattern. Sew three piece Bs together to make a unit (Fig. 15–14). Press the seams in one direction. Make eight identical units.

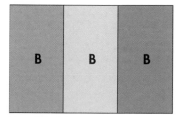
Fig. 15–14

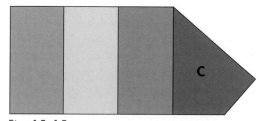
Fig. 15–15

Sew a piece C to one end of each of the B units (Fig. 15–15). Mark the seam allowances on the wrong side of the fabric of octagon A (Fig. 15–16). Sew the new unit to a straight edge of the octagon or piece A (Fig. 15–17). Sew only to the seam allowance marked line and not through all the seam allowance. Sew the next unit to a straight side of the octagon A, and then sew the seam connecting the straight end of the unit with piece C (Fig. 15–18). You are sewing a set-in point so take care in pinning and sewing. Continue adding units around the octagon (A) until a Wedding Ring Tile unit is complete.

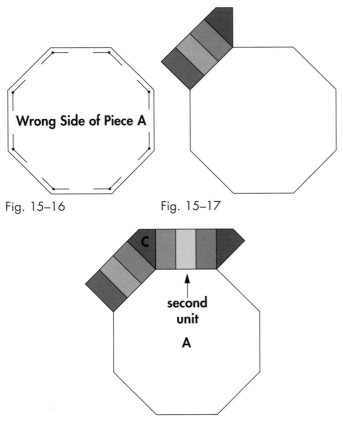

Fig. 15–16   Fig. 15–17

Fig. 15–18

When all of the Wedding Ring Tile units are complete, follow the directions in the Sets section for sewing an Octagonal Set (page 17) to complete the quilt top. Square E and triangle F are used to join the octagon units together.

BRIDAL STAIRWAY

Use this sashing with plain blocks or appliquéd blocks. Bridal Stairway is from the 1930s and is very pleasing when the rectangles in the sashings are pastel prints and the small triangles are the same fabric as the block background fabric (Photo 69).

Pattern: 4" wide sashing to fit a 9" block, page 136.

Worksheet: Bridal Stairway sashing, page 118.

Sizing of Sashing: Make a paper quilt (see page 5) to determine the number of block units needed for

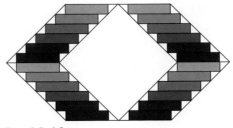

Fig. 15–19

the size quilt desired. The diagonal sashing sections are sewn to four sides of the block to make a hexagonal block unit as shown in Figure 15–19. A block unit measures 12¾" up and down and 24" across. The numbers of each piece needed for one block unit are given under the cutting instructions.

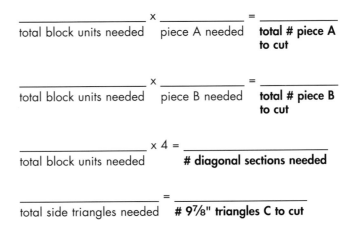

$$\underline{\hspace{3cm}} \times \underline{\hspace{3cm}} = \underline{\hspace{3cm}}$$
total block units needed   piece A needed   **total # piece A to cut**

$$\underline{\hspace{3cm}} \times \underline{\hspace{3cm}} = \underline{\hspace{3cm}}$$
total block units needed   piece B needed   **total # piece B to cut**

$$\underline{\hspace{3cm}} \times 4 = \underline{\hspace{3cm}}$$
total block units needed   **# diagonal sections needed**

$$\underline{\hspace{3cm}} = \underline{\hspace{3cm}}$$
total side triangles needed   **# 9⅞" triangles C to cut**

Part of the blocks for this quilt are setting blocks with the rest being blocks used to make a block unit. Count the number of squares on the paper quilt to determine the number of 9½" squares to cut.

Cutting: Below are the numbers of each piece needed for one hexagonal block unit.

- cut pattern piece A
   24 or 24 rectangles that measure 1⁵⁄₁₆" x 4½"
- cut pattern piece B – 48

From the same fabric as the 9½" blocks, cut the number of large 9⅞" triangles (C) that are needed for the sides of the quilt top. Be sure the straight of the fabric grain is along the long side of the triangles. Cut four 7⅝" corner (D) triangles.

Sewing: Sew a triangle (B) to each end of a rectangle (A). Make two diagonal sashing sections by sewing these units together (Fig. 15–20a). Match and pin before sewing. To make the other two diagonal sashing sections (Fig. 15–20b), flip the B triangles on both ends. Sew the total number of section needed.

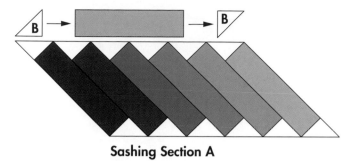

Sashing Section A

Fig. 15–20a

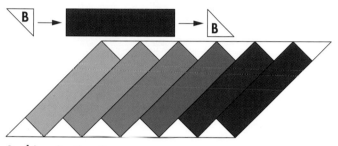

Sashing Section B

Fig. 15–20b

Photo 69. Detail, STAIRWAY TO ROSES by the author. Bridal Stairway sashing.

On the wrong side of the 9½" blocks, mark ¼" seam allowances on the two opposite corners (Fig. 15–21). Match the seam allowance corner on a sashing section A with the marked seam lines of the block. Sew from one corner mark to the other corner mark (Fig. 15–22). Sew a sashing section B to the side of the block (Fig. 15–23). Match the diagonal ends of the two sashing sections and pin. Sew from the block marked corner out to the sashing edge (Fig. 15–24, page 76). Sew two more sashing sections to the other sides of the blocks (Fig. 15–25, page 76).

For a straight hexagonal set, sew the hexagonal block units in rows the desired length of the quilt top (Fig. 15–26, page 76).

On one of the rows, set in C triangles on the quilt top side and 9½" squares on the other side of the hexagonal block units (Fig. 15–27, page 76).

seam line marked

wrong side of 9½" block

seam line marked

Fig. 15–21

Section A

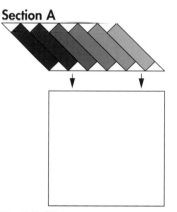

Fig. 15–22

Section A

Section B

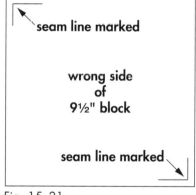

Fig. 15–23

Continue completion of the quilt top by adding hexagonal block unit rows and triangles (Fig. 15–28, page 76).

In Figure 15–29, page 76, this variation shows the hexagonal block row (outlined) going diagonally across the quilt top. Sewing the rows is the same as described for the hexagonal set except the length of each row is different. Refer to your paper quilt to determine the number of hexagonal block units to put in each row. Since there are many partial block units, the easiest construction method may be to finish the hexagonal block units and then cut those units to fit where they are needed.

Fig. 15–24

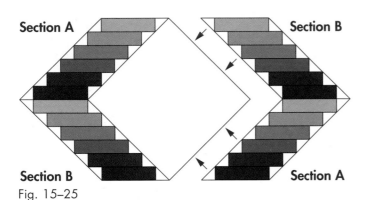

Fig. 15–25

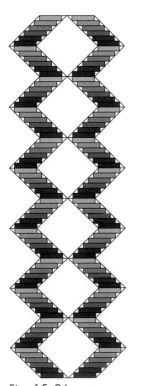

Fig. 15–26

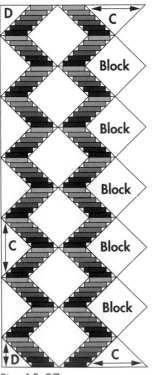

Fig. 15–27

Fig. 15–28

Fig. 15–29

ATTIC WINDOW

The Attic Window sashing gives the illusion of the block sitting in a window frame. The illusion is created by having sashing on only two sides, with one of those sashing strips being lighter than the other. This sashing makes a good showcase for either pieced or appliquéd blocks (Photo 70).

STRAIGHT

This sashing is used for either squares or rectangles.

Pattern: None

Worksheet: Straight Attic Windows sashing, page 119.

Sets & Sashings for Quilts – Phyllis D. Miller

Photo 70. Detail, GRANDMA ALWAYS HAD FLOWERS IN HER WINDOW by Karen S. Riggins. Straight Attic Window sashing.

Cutting: The sashing strips can be rotary cut. Cut all of the sashing strips either across the fabric width or along the selvage.

Sewing: In the corner where the sashing miter will be, mark a ¼" seam line on the wrong side of the block (Photo 71). Light and dark placement of the sashing strips is your choice; the dark represents the shadow in the frame. Place a dark fabric strip on the block with right sides together and with the leftover fabric at the corner of the block where the miter will be.

Photo 71.

Photo 72.

Sew on the block side from the top of the strip to the corner seam marked on the block (Photo 72); backstitch.

Place the light fabric strip on the other side of the

Photo 73.

block to be framed with the leftover fabric overlapping the dark leftover fabric (Photo 73). Start sewing at the marked corner of the block, backstitch, and finish sewing the strip to the block.

Take the block unit to the ironing board. Press the seam allowances toward the sashing pieces. Place the block right side up and the dark sashing strip spread out straight on the ironing board. Take the light fabric strip, fold it under and align the light

Sizing of Sashing: Decide how many blocks you need to make the quilt. This will be determined by the size of the quilt. Each block is framed on two sides to make a block unit (Fig. 16–1). The sashing width can be narrow or wide depending on the look you want.

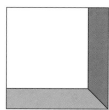

Fig. 16–1

$$\frac{}{\text{total \# blocks}} = \frac{}{\textbf{\# light strips to cut}}$$

$$\frac{}{\text{total \# blocks}} = \frac{}{\textbf{\# dark strips to cut}}$$

$$\frac{}{\text{sashing width}} + \tfrac{1}{2}" = \frac{}{\textbf{width to cut sashing strips}}$$

$$\frac{}{\text{block width}} + \frac{}{\text{2 x sashing width}} = \frac{}{\textbf{length to cut sashing strips}}$$

fabric strip edges with the dark sashing strip edges (Photo 74). Press where the fold is to make a miter (Photo 75).

Photo 74.

Photo 75.

Photo 76.

Photo 77.

Pin the two sashing strips together along the sashing end and in the excess fabric area (Photo 76).

Fold the block and the dark sashing strip over to line up the two sashing edges (Photo 77).

Start sewing at the block corner where the sashing strip was backstitched. Sew on the crease line out to the sashing edge (Photo 78).

Turn the unit over and check to see if the miter is right (Photo 79). The block and the sashing should lie flat. Trim the excess sashing fabric away, leaving a ¼" seam allowance. Add sashing strips to all of the blocks in the same manner.

Finish the quilt top by following the directions for the Straight Set on page 10.

Photo 78.

Photo 79.

DIAMOND

The panes in this Attic Window are diamond shaped and can be either 45° or 60° diamonds (Photo 80).

Photo 80. DREAM GARDEN
by the author. Diamond Attic Window sashing.

Pattern: None. Directions are given for making templates for any size diamond pane and the sashing.

Worksheet: Diamond Attic Window sashing, page 120.

Sizing of Sashing: Make a paper quilt (see page 5) to determine the number of diamond panes needed. The supplies needed to make the templates are a 6" wide long ruler, pencil, eraser, accurate 45° or 60° diamond template, poster board, and a piece of freezer paper.

In the center of the piece of freezer paper, draw a long vertical line down the paper. Lay a line of the ruler on the drawn line, and draw a long horizontal line across the center (Fig. 16–2). Decide how long the diamond will be and make a mark that is half of this length up from the center and down from the center (Fig. 16–3). For example, for a 9" long diamond, make marks 4½" above and below the center line.

Place the diamond template with the ends lined up with the length mark and the pencil line (Fig. 16–4). On the inside of the diamond template, draw a line along both sides of the top of the diamond (Fig. 16-5) and repeat at the bottom mark (Fig. 16–6). Place the ruler edge next to one of the drawn lines, lined up exactly with one of the diamond lines. Draw a line along the ruler edge from above the length mark to the horizontal pencil line (Fig. 16–7). Draw lines in the same way for all 4 sides of the diamond. The lines should meet or cross exactly at the center line (Fig. 16–8).

line mark

Fig. 16–2

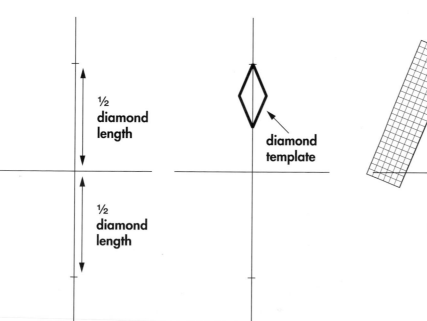

½ diamond length

½ diamond length

diamond template

Fig. 16–3   Fig. 16–4

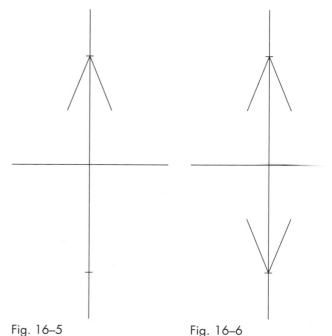

Fig. 16–5   Fig. 16–6

Fig. 16–7   Fig. 16–8

Decide what width the sashing strips will be. A 1½" width is a good choice but it can be more narrow or wider. On the right side of the diamond top, draw a line the sashing width from the diamond edge (Fig. 16–9). Draw another line the same distance from the diamond edge at the right bottom half of the diamond (Fig. 16–10) and erase the excess lines.

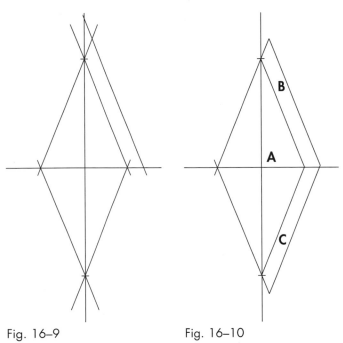

Fig. 16–9   Fig. 16–10

Templates can now be made by carefully cutting out the diamond and sashing patterns and ironing the freezer paper patterns to poster board. For the diamond (A), use a craft knife or single edge razor blade to cut out the diamond to make a window

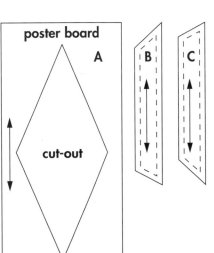

Fig. 16–11

template. For the sashing templates, add ¼" seam allowances to all sides of the freezer paper pattern and cut out to make the templates (Fig. 16–11). The diamond shape is template A, the top of the diamond sashing is template B and

the bottom of the diamond sashing is template C. It is easier to have two templates than using the template B reversed.

A half diamond template D and a long half diamond (F) are needed to complete the quilt top and these can be made by using the cut out diamond template (A) to draw two diamond shapes on freezer paper. Divide one diamond across the center and add seam allowances to make template D. Divide the other diamond in half lengthwise and add seam allowances to make template F (Fig. 16 – 12).

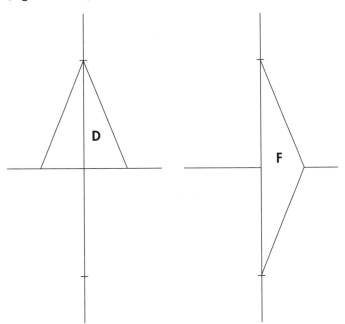

Fig. 16–12

Each diamond is sashed on one side with the top sashing dark and the bottom sashing light. This makes one diamond unit (Fig. 16–13). Count the half diamonds (F) that are on the left side of the quilt top as full diamonds (A) when determining the units needed. The right side of the quilt is easier if the full diamond unit is made and then the quilt edge is cut straight removing part of the diamond units. There is some fabric waste but fewer templates are needed if constructed this way.

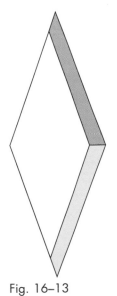

Fig. 16–13

_____	+ _____	= _____
diamonds (A) needed	half diamonds (D) at bottom	**# dark sashing (B) to cut**
_____	+ _____	= _____
diamonds(A) needed	half diamonds (D) at top	**# light sashing (B) to cut**

Cutting: Use template A as a window to frame the part of the fabric you want to view in the pane (Photo 81). With a fabric marking pencil or pen, mark the diamond shape on the fabric. Add ¼" seam allowances and cut out. Place the diamond on a design wall to help in deciding how to cut the next diamond. When all the diamonds and half diamonds have been cut, cut all of the dark sashing

pieces using template B. Place the sashing pieces on the design wall. Cut all of the light sashing pieces using template C and place these on the design wall. Cut and add more pieces if and where needed.

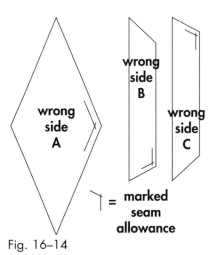

Photo 81.

Mark the seam allowances on the wrong sides of the fabric pieces (A, B, C as shown in Figure 16–14).

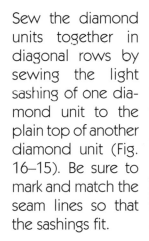

wrong side A

wrong side B

wrong side C

⌐ = **marked seam allowance**

Fig. 16–14

Sewing: Carefully pin a dark sashing piece B to the top right side of a diamond, right sides of the fabric facing. Sew exactly to the marked corner on the sashing piece and backstitch (Photo 82).

Pin the light sashing piece C to the bottom right side of the diamond. Sew this piece by starting exactly at the marked corner of the sashing piece (Photo 83).

Match the ends of the light and dark sashing pieces and starting at the diamond, sew the two sashing pieces together. Press the seams toward the dark sashing piece and away from the light sashing piece. The diamond unit should look like the one in Photo 84. Place the diamond units back on the design wall as they are finished.

Photo 82.

Photo 83.

Sew the diamond units together in diagonal rows by sewing the light sashing of one diamond unit to the plain top of another diamond unit (Fig. 16–15). Be sure to mark and match the seam lines so that the sashings fit.

Photo 84.

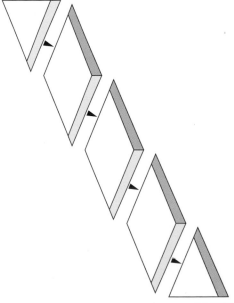

Fig. 16–15

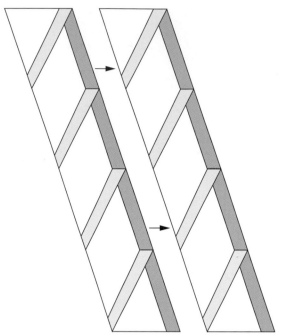

Fig. 16–16

Sew two rows together after carefully matching and pinning where the sashings met (Fig. 16–16). When the all of the units are sewn together to make a top, trim the right side of the piece to give it a straight edge (Fig. 16–17).

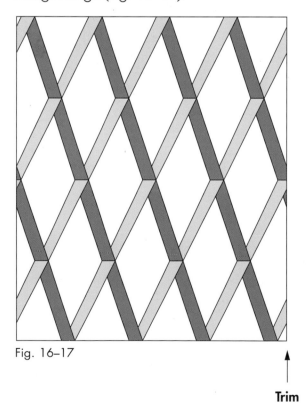

Fig. 16–17

Trim

FRAMING

Framing is the addition of fabric strips to all sides of the block and is used either to emphasize the block, to make the blocks larger, or, in the case of blocks made by several people, to make all of the blocks the same size. The small variation from one block to another is not visually noticeable. The width of the framing can be as narrow as ⅛" or as wide as 2".

Photo 85. FLOWERS OF CINCINNATI
by the Quilt Pros – Bonnie Browning, June Culvey, Donna McDade, Paul McDade, Jenny Perry, Karen S. Riggins, Dee Rosing, Marie Salazar, Ruth Ann Thompson, and the author. Butted Corners Framing.

PIPED FRAMING

The piping described here is fabric with no cording although corded piping could be used.

Pattern: None

Sizing of Sashing: This framing will be very narrow with ⅛" piping showing around the block.

$$\underset{\text{block width}}{\underline{}} + \underset{\text{½" for seam}}{\underline{}} = \underset{\textbf{length to cut piping strips}}{\underline{}}$$

$$\underset{\text{total \# blocks}}{\underline{}} \times 4 = \underset{\textbf{\# piping strips to cut}}{\underline{}}$$

Cutting: The piping strips should be cut ¾" wide across the grain of the fabric. If you want ¼" piping, cut the piping strips 1" wide.

Sewing: Fold the piping strips in half lengthwise and press. Place the cut edge of the piping strip along the block's top edge and sew using a ¼" seam allowance (Fig. 17–1). Sew the piping strip to the top and to the bottom of the block first and then to the two sides. Trim, if needed.

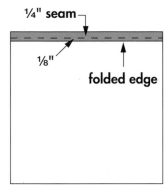

¼" seam

⅛"

folded edge

Fig. 17–1

The block framed with piping (Fig. 17–2) is now ready to be used in the same way as any un-framed block.

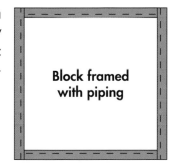

Block framed with piping

Fig. 17–2

BUTTED CORNERS FRAMING

Framing blocks with butted corners is a good, and easy, choice when using either solid fabric or a print fabric with a small design. The framing can be the same color for all the blocks, especially if other sashing will be used, or can be alternated with light fabric to frame one block and dark fabric to frame the next.

Pattern: None

Sizing of Sashing: Decide how wide you would like the framing. The width can vary from ½" to 3", or wider for larger blocks.

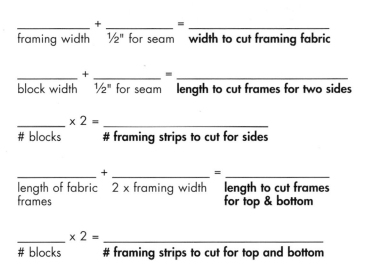

$$\underline{\hspace{2cm}}_{\text{framing width}} + \underline{\hspace{1.5cm}}_{\text{½" for seam}} = \underline{\hspace{2cm}}_{\textbf{width to cut framing fabric}}$$

$$\underline{\hspace{2cm}}_{\text{block width}} + \underline{\hspace{1.5cm}}_{\text{½" for seam}} = \underline{\hspace{2cm}}_{\textbf{length to cut frames for two sides}}$$

$$\underline{\hspace{1.5cm}}_{\text{\# blocks}} \times 2 = \underline{\hspace{2cm}}_{\textbf{\# framing strips to cut for sides}}$$

$$\underline{\hspace{2cm}}_{\substack{\text{length of fabric}\\\text{frames}}} + \underline{\hspace{1.5cm}}_{\text{2 x framing width}} = \underline{\hspace{2cm}}_{\substack{\textbf{length to cut frames}\\\textbf{for top \& bottom}}}$$

$$\underline{\hspace{1.5cm}}_{\text{\# blocks}} \times 2 = \underline{\hspace{2cm}}_{\textbf{\# framing strips to cut for top and bottom}}$$

Cutting: Rotary cut strips across the fabric grain to make framing strips in the required numbers for the sides, top, and bottom of the block.

Sewing: Sew a short framing strip to each side of the block (Fig. 17–3). Press the seams toward the framing. Sew a long framing strip to the top and the bottom of the block and frames (Fig. 17–4).

The framed block is now ready to be used in the same way an unframed block would be used to make the quilt top.

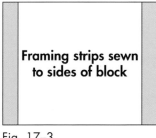

Framing strips sewn to sides of block

Fig. 17–3

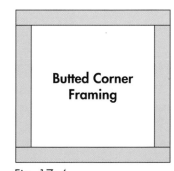

Butted Corner Framing

Fig. 17–4

MITERED FRAMING

The corners of mitered framing are joined at a 45° angle. Mitering can be used with any fabric. Striped or directional fabric should be mitered to make a pleasing frame Fig. 17–5).

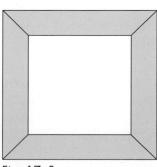

Fig. 17–5

Pattern: None

Sizing of Sashing: All four sides of the block are framed and the size of the framing will be whatever is pleasing or, in the case of striped fabric, the width of the printed stripe or design.

$$\frac{}{\text{block width}} + \frac{}{\text{2 x framing width}} = \frac{}{\textbf{length to cut framing strips}}$$

$$\frac{}{\text{total \# blocks}} \times 4 = \frac{}{\textbf{\# framing strips to cut}}$$

Cutting: If striped fabric is used, cut the framing strips so the center of a design in the fabric stripe is always in the middle of the strip. This will ensure that the design in all four corners is the same.

Sewing: Mark the ¼" seam allowance on all four corners of the block. If striped fabric is used, match the center of the framing strip with the center of the block and pin. Sew the framing strip to the block from corner seam mark to corner seam mark, backstitching at both ends. Sew all four framing strips to the block in the same manner. Refer to the directions for completing the miter by following the directions for the Attic Windows sashing on page 77.

The blocks are now ready to be used, just as unframed blocks, to make a quilt top.

HEXAGONAL OR OCTAGONAL FRAMING

Framing hexagon or octagon blocks is often a good way to emphasize the block shape. This is especially true for appliqué blocks in these shapes.

Pattern: None

Sizing of Sashing: On freezer paper, draw a hexagon or octagon block the same size as the finished block you have. A hexagon block will be used in these examples.

Decide the finished width for the framing. With a ruler, add this amount to each side of the hexagon (Fig. 17–6). Use a ruler to draw lines across this added width at the hexagon points (Fig. 17–7).

Add ¼" seam allowances on each side of this frame pattern (Fig. 17–8). Cut out the pattern piece and iron it to poster board or some other material to make a template.

$$\frac{}{\text{\# blocks to be framed}} \times 6 = \frac{}{\textbf{\# framing pieces to cut}}$$

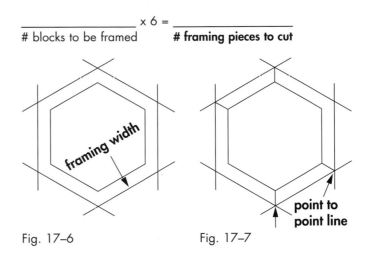

Fig. 17–6   Fig. 17–7

If the block is an octagon, multiply by eight in the above formula.

Cutting: Cut all the framing pieces on the same straight grain of the fabric, either across the fabric width or lengthwise with the selvage.

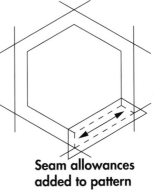

Sewing: Mark ¼" seam allowances on all the corners of the wrong side of the block (Fig. 17–9).

Seam allowances added to pattern

Fig. 17–8

Pin a framing piece to the block, right sides together. Pin at the corners. Sew from one corner seam mark to the next corner seam mark. Backstitch at the beginning and ending of each seam. Attach all the framing pieces in the same way. Pin the ends of two framing strips and sew from the block out to the edge of the frame to sew the miters.

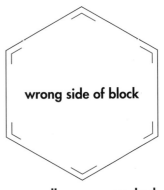

wrong side of block

seam allowances marked
Fig. 17–9

When all of the framing pieces have been joined, the block is ready to use in the same way an unframed block would be used (Fig. 17–10). Follow the assembly directions for either the Hexagonal Set (page 12) or the Octagonal Set (page 17) to finish the quilt top.

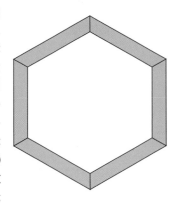

Fig. 17–10

SKEWED FRAMING

Adding long, skinny triangles to all four sides of a block will cause the block to appear skewed or slanted. Use this framing to add pizzazz to a quilt. One or more skewed frames can be added in the same or varied widths. Anything goes! (Photo 86)

Pattern: None

Photo 86. BLOOMIN' IN THE WIND by Judy Robinson. Skewed framing. Photo by maker.

Sizing, Cutting and Sewing of Framing: Since the Skewed framing is a cut-and-sew-as-you-go method, the directions will be given to add two frames. An 8" block will be used in this example. Substitute the width of your blocks for this number.

❀ The edges of a Skewed framed block will have bias edges and will need to be handled with care. If you do not want to work with bias edges, draft templates for the long triangles.

Frame 1: For each block, cut four rectangles the width of the block plus seam allowances and as wide as you would like the wide end of the long triangle plus seam allowances. (Example: 1½" x 8½")

Sew a rectangle to one side of the block and press the seam away from the block (Photo 87). Sew rectangles to the other three sides of the block in the same way. Be sure to line up the end of the rectangle with the block edge. The fabric rectangle will overlap another rectangle ¼".

Photo 87.

Use a wide ruler and rotary cutter to cut the long triangle. Lay the ruler edge at the top of one side of the fabric rectangle and align the ruler so that it lies diagonally across the rectangle and has a ¼" mark on the ruler over the corner of the block (Photo 88).

Photo 88.

Cut along the ruler edge. A small sliver of the end of the rectangle on the side will be cut off. Cut all four rectangles exactly the same to look like the block in Photo 89, page 86. Check to see if the new block is square and, if needed, square up the block.

Photo 89.

Photo 90.

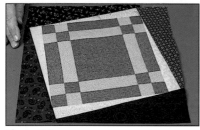
Photo 91.

Frame 2: Measure the width of the new block. Cut rectangles this length and the width wanted for this framing, (example: 3" wide x 9⅜" long). Sew these new rectangles to all four sides of the skew-framed block in the same manner as described for Frame 1. If the wide end of the first long triangle is on the right of the block, place the ruler so that the new triangle cut will be wide on the left side of the block (Photo 90). Cut the other rectangles the same and square up the blocks.

To add more Skewed frames, measure the width of the new block and add the new frames following the same directions as for Frame 2 (Photo 91).

When the frame has been skewed to your satisfaction, the new blocks are ready to be used in a set of your choice to finish the quilt top.

APPLIQUÉD SASHINGS

The variety of designs that can be used in appliquéd sashings are numerous and only limited by the imagination. The appliqué designs can run the gamut from abstract geometric designs to fancy florals. Appliqué designs can be used on plain or pieced sashings.

The Appliquéd Sashings shown here were chosen to give you a starting place for adding this elegant touch to your quilts. The instructions under the Lady Finger sashing can be used with any appliqué design to make the appliqué designs fit any sashing size.

A paper pattern for placement of the appliqué pieces on the sashing will be needed. Decide what width the sashing will be. The size of the appliqué design will help determine this. Approximately one-third of the finished block size is a good guide to size the appliquéd sashing.

Cut a piece of paper the finished width and length of the sashing piece plus the corner connecting square (Fig. 18–1). Add the square, which is the same as the finished width, even though it may not actually be a separate square. The square is needed for continuity of the design around the corner.

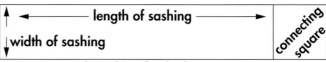
Paper cut exactly sashing finished size + connecting square
Fig. 18–1

For designs that are straight on the sashing, fold the paper in half lengthwise to find the center for placement of the design. Placement for other designs can be made by folding paper. By folding the paper in equal parts, the appliqué design can be drawn to fit the sashing. The appliqué sashings and patterns that follow will have instructions for the paper folding for each different design.

Make a paper quilt (page 5) to determine the number of sashing strips and connecting squares needed.

Use the formulas for the type sashing chosen to figure the number of sashing strips and/or connecting squares to cut. For example, if the appliqué design will be used on a one piece sashing with connecting block, use the directions on page 40 for that sashing.

LADY FINGER

This sashing from as early as the 1840s is usually found with blocks as shown in Figure 18–2. It has also been called Grandmother's Engagement Ring, Whig's Defeat, Missouri Beauty, and others. The sashing for the Lady Finger is wide because the blocks are usually larger than 20". The fingers can be all from the same fabric or varied fabrics and shades. (Photo 92)

Fig. 18–2

Pattern: Page 135 to fit 12" wide sashing.

Worksheet: Lady Finger sashing, page 121.

Sizing of Sashing: The Lady Finger pattern is for a 12" wide sashing. To make a more narrow or wider sashing, multiply ⅓ of the block size by two to find the width. The finger pattern can be enlarged or reduced on a copy machine to fit a different width. The fingers are centered across the width on the sashing.

Cut a piece of paper the finished width and length of the sashing strip. Fold the paper in half across the middle to find the placement position of the center finger. Use a black permanent marking pen to trace the Lady Finger design at the center of the paper (Fig. 18–3). The paper placement pattern is now ready to be placed under the sashing fabric and traced onto the fabric.

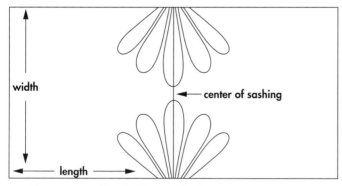

Placement of Lady Finger design on paper pattern

Fig. 18–3

Photo 92. GRANDMOTHER'S ENGAGEMENT RING by Lucy Ann Grady. Lady Finger sashing.

_____ _____ x 2 = _____		
total # sashing strips		**total # A to cut**
_____ x 4 = _____		
total # sashing strips		**total # B to cut**
_____ x 4 = _____		
total # sashing strips		**total # C to cut**

Cutting: There are two sets of fingers on each sashing strip. Add seam allowances to the patterns. For each sashing:

- cut pattern piece A – 2
- cut pattern piece B – 4
- cut pattern piece C – 4

Sewing: Place the appliqué pieces on the marked placement lines on the sashing strip and appliqué in place.

After the appliqué has been finished, assemble the quilt top following the directions in the Sets section for the set that you have chosen.

SCROLLING VINE WITH FLOWERS AND LEAVES

Simple traditional flowers and leaves are attached to a curving vine in this appliquéd sashing. Other flowers and leaves can be substituted, if desired. (Photo 93)

Photo 93. Detail, DOUBLE NINE PATCH
by the author. Scrolling Vine with Flowers and Leaves sashing.

Pattern: Page 137 will fit a 4" wide sashing.

Worksheet: Scrolling Vine with Flowers and Leaves sashing, page 122.

Sizing of Sashing: Refer to the directions for cutting paper the finished size of sashing plus the connecting block (Fig. 18–1, page 86). To make the curving vine fit, fold the sizing paper in half with one end coming over to the connecting square line. Fold in half again (Fig. 18–4). Open up the paper and fold in half lengthwise and then in half again (Fig. 18–5).

second fold →	center first fold →	second fold →	connecting square

Fig. 18–4

Section 1   Section 2   fold lines

Fig. 18–5

On the first section, draw a gentle curve from the corner of the middle fold down to the next line (the center fold of section 1) and then back up to the middle fold (Fig. 18–6). Fold in half the whole length of the two sections. Fold again on the fold line that divides the two sections. Trace the curved line which should be on the upper half of the second section (Fig. 18–7). Unfold the paper and the lines should look like those in Figure 18–8.

Section 1   **Section 2**

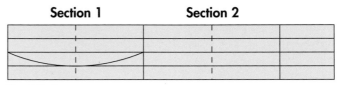

Fig. 18–6

center fold   fold line

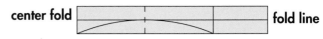

Fig. 18–7

Section 1   **Section 2**

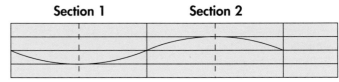

Fig. 18–8

To complete the placement pattern for the Scrolling Vine, make templates for the 3 pattern pieces. Use a small ruler to make the vine ¼" wide. Place the flower template in the center of the connecting block and draw around it (Fig. 18–9). Then place the templates along the vine and fill in with leaves and flowers until the effect is pleasing. Extend the vine into the connecting square (Fig. 18–10). Go over the lines with a black permanent marker and the placement pattern is now ready to be used to trace the design onto the sashing fabric.

Section 1   **Section 2**

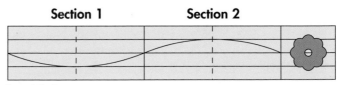

Fig. 18–9

Section 1   **Section 2**

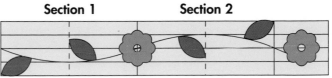

Fig. 18–10

To determine the number of pieces needed, make a paper quilt (page 5). Use the following formulas to determine the numbers of each appliqué pattern piece to cut. Count the pieces on your placement pattern and connecting squares to fill in the numbers.

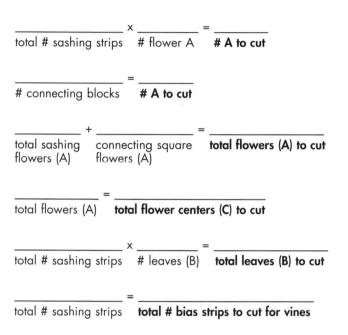

_____ x _____ = _____
total # sashing strips   # flower A   **# A to cut**

_____ = _____
# connecting blocks   **# A to cut**

_____ + _____ = _____
total sashing   connecting square   **total flowers (A) to cut**
flowers (A)   flowers (A)

_____ = _____
total flowers (A)   **total flower centers (C) to cut**

_____ x _____ = _____
total # sashing strips   # leaves (B)   **total leaves (B) to cut**

_____ = _____
total # sashing strips   **total # bias strips to cut for vines**

Cutting: Add seam allowances to the appliqué pieces before cutting. The bias strips for the vines should be cut with ¼" seam allowances added or ¾" wide. Be sure to cut the strips long enough to extend into the connecting block and to go under the flower.

Sewing: Place the appliqué pieces on the traced lines on the sashing strip and appliqué in place. After the appliqué has been finished, assemble the quilt top following the directions for the one strip sashing with plain connecting blocks on page 40, and the directions for the set that you have chosen from the Sets section.

FEATHER

Inlaid or reverse appliqué is used to make this straight Feather Sashing with Hearts in the connecting blocks. It can be sewn with the sashing in the same fabric as the background of the block and a dark fabric for the feather or reversed with the darker fabric as the sashing and the feathers being a lighter fabric (Photo 94).

Photo 94. Detail, A TOUCH OF ROMANCE
Sashing by Janice Walden. Block by the author. Feather sashing.

Pattern: Page 137 will fit a 12" block and is 3" wide. The pattern can be enlarged or decreased on a copy machine to fit other size blocks.

Worksheet: Feather sashing, page 123.

Sizing of Sashing: Make a paper quilt (see page 5) to determine the number of sashing strips and connecting blocks needed for the type of set chosen.

_____ = _____
total # sashings   **# 3½" x 12½" sashing pieces to cut**

_____ = _____
total sashing pieces   **# 3½" x 12½" pieces from Feather fabric**

_____ = _____
total connecting squares   **# 3½" squares to cut from both fabrics**

Cutting: The strips can be rotary cut on the straight grain of the fabric.

Sewing: Mark the Feather design on the sashing fabric using a fabric marking pen or pencil. Baste the sashing fabric (on top) and the feather fabric (on bottom) together. Baste around the feather and heart shapes so the two fabrics won't slip while appliquéing.

With small, sharp scissors, cut out the inside of the shape leaving a small seam allowance and clipping when necessary. Turn under the seam allowance and, using thread to match the sashing fabric, appliqué around the Feather and Heart shapes. When the reverse appliqué has been completed, trim away the excess Feather (bottom) fabric.

When all of the sashing strips and connecting blocks have been completed, assemble the quilt top by following the directions for the one strip with plain connecting sashing (page 40) and for the chosen set.

FANCY FLORAL

Because of the numerous flowers and leaves on this sashing, this style should be used with a large block (Photo 95).

Photo 95. Detail, THE KENTUCKY BEAUTY by Mary Andra Holmes. Fancy Floral sashing.

Pattern: Page 138 is for an 18" block. The sashing finishes 6" wide.

Worksheet: Fancy Floral sashing, page 124.

Sizing of Sashing: Make a paper quilt (see page 5) to determine the number of sashing strips and connecting blocks needed.

_____ x 7 = _____
total # sashing strips   **# piece A to cut**

_____ x 7 = _____
total # sashing strips   **# piece B to cut**

_____ x 21 = _____
total # sashing strips   **# piece C to cut**

_____ = _____
total # sashing strips   **# ¾" x 24" bias strips to cut**

_____ = _____
total # connecting blocks   **# piece D to cut**

_____ = _____
total # connecting blocks   **# piece E to cut**

_____ x 4 = _____
total # connecting blocks   **# piece C to cut**

_____ + _____ = _____
piece C for sashing strips   piece C for blocks   **total # piece C to cut**

Cutting: Cut the number of sashing strips and connecting blocks from the sashing background fabric. Add seam allowances to the Fancy Florals patterns and cut out the appliqué pieces. Cut the required number of bias strips for the stem. The pieces are cut extra long to ensure having sufficient length when appliquéing.

Sewing: Appliqué the stem first. Leave the bias strips loose at the end of the sashing strip so it can be appliquéd onto the connecting blocks. The stem should finish ¼" wide. Appliqué the flowers, flower centers, and leaves on the sashing strips and the connecting blocks. The stems for the flowers and leaves are embroidered using a stem stitch (Fig. 18–11).

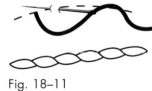

Fig. 18–11

When the appliqué is completed, assemble the quilt top following the directions in Part 2 for the set you have chosen.

LEAVES

This sashing shows how a simple appliqué shape can be used to create an exciting look, especially when used with geometric pieced blocks or to echo a shape from an appliqué block (Photo 96). The leaves could also be placed along a curving vine (see page 88).

Pattern: Page 141 for 4" by 12" sashing and connecting block.

Worksheet: Leaves sashing, page 125.

Sizing of Sashing: Make a paper quilt (see page 5) to determine the number of sashing strips and connecting blocks needed.

| _____ | x 16 = | _____ |
| total # sashing strips | | **# leaves for sashings to cut** |

| _____ | = | _____ |
| total # sashing strips | | **# ¾" x 14" bias strips to cut** |

| _____ | x 4 – | _____ |
| total # connecting blocks | | **# leaves for blocks to cut** |

| _____ | + | _____ | – | _____ |
| leaves for sashings | | leaves for connecting blocks | | **total # leaves to cut** |

Cutting: Add seam allowances to the finished size (4½" x 12½") of the sashing and cut as many as needed. Cut the required number of bias strips for the stem down the center of each sashing.

Add seam allowances to the leaf pattern and cut the number of leaves needed. Consider using a large number of different fabrics to give a realistic look.

Photo 96. Detail, ORCHID IMPRESSIONS
Block by Marie Salazar. Sashing by author.
Leaves sashing.

Sewing: Mark the placement of the stem and leaves on the sashing and connecting block fabric (Fig. 18–12). The stem finishes ¼" wide and the stem should be appliquéd first.

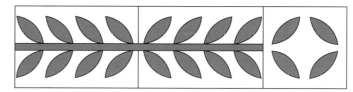

Fig. 18–12

After all of the leaves have been appliquéd in place, the sashings and blocks are ready to be used to assemble the quilt top following the directions for the set chosen.

WORKSHEETS FOR SASHINGS

Alternating Snowball Block Sashing – Straight Set Worksheet

Sets & Sashings for Quilts – Phyllis D. Miller

Plain Strip Sashing with Pieced Connecting Blocks – Straight Set Worksheet

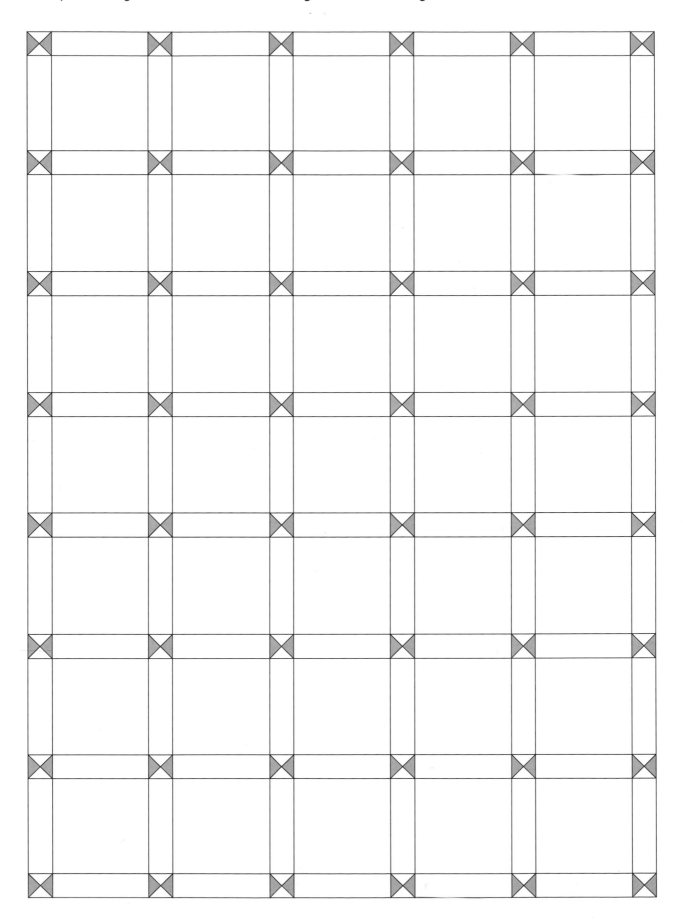

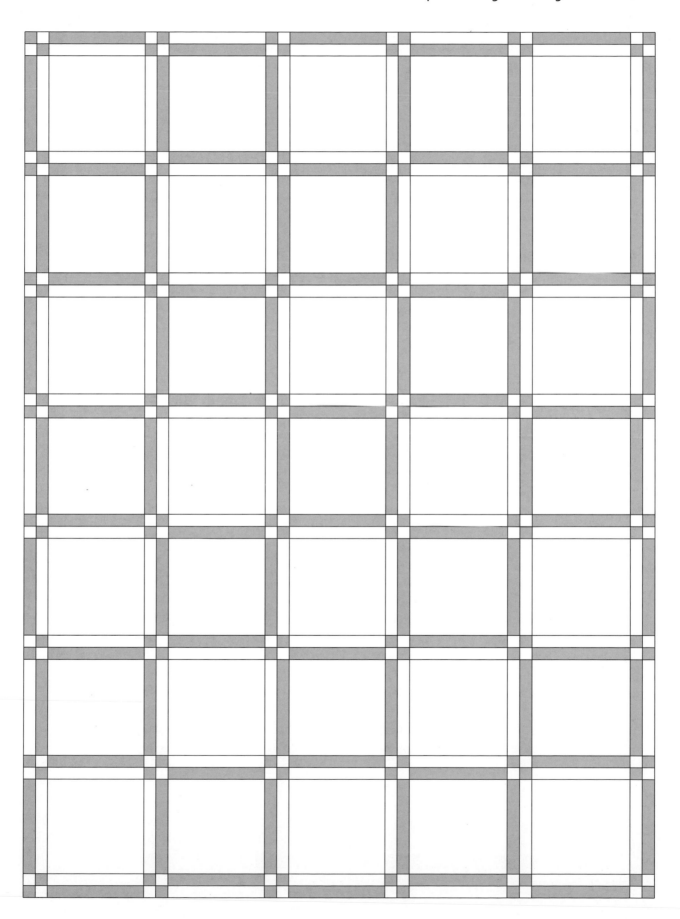

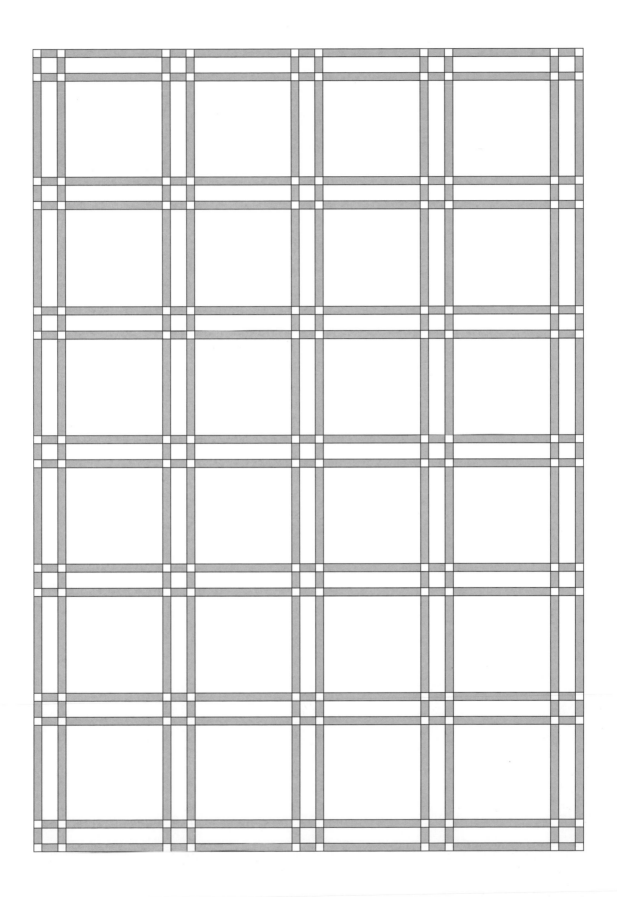

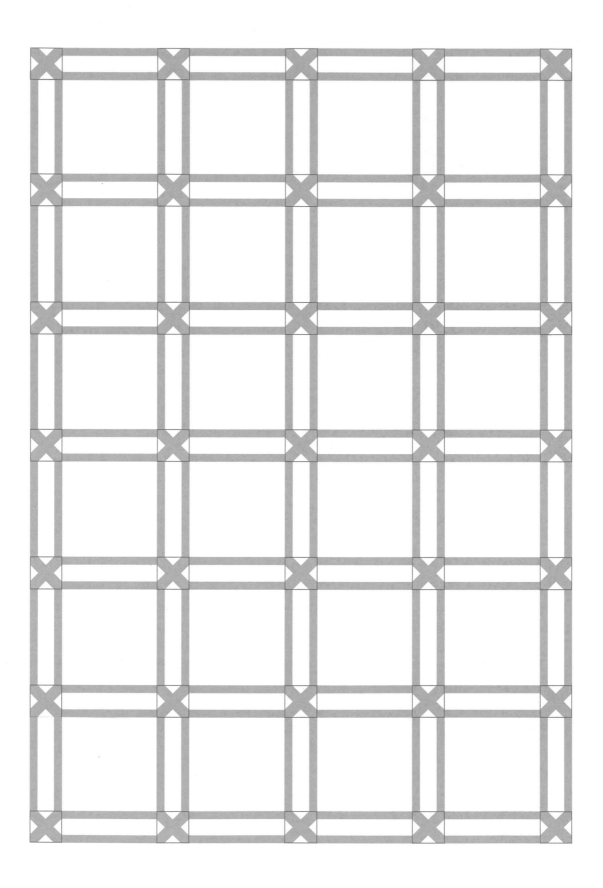

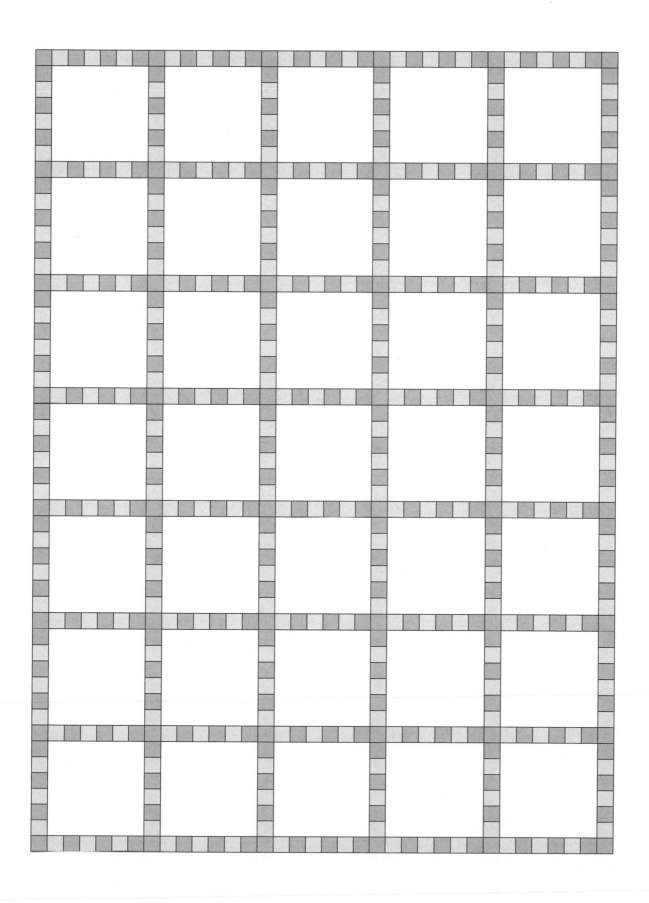

Sets & Sashings for Quilts – Phyllis D. Miller

Sets & Sashings for Quilts – Phyllis D. Miller

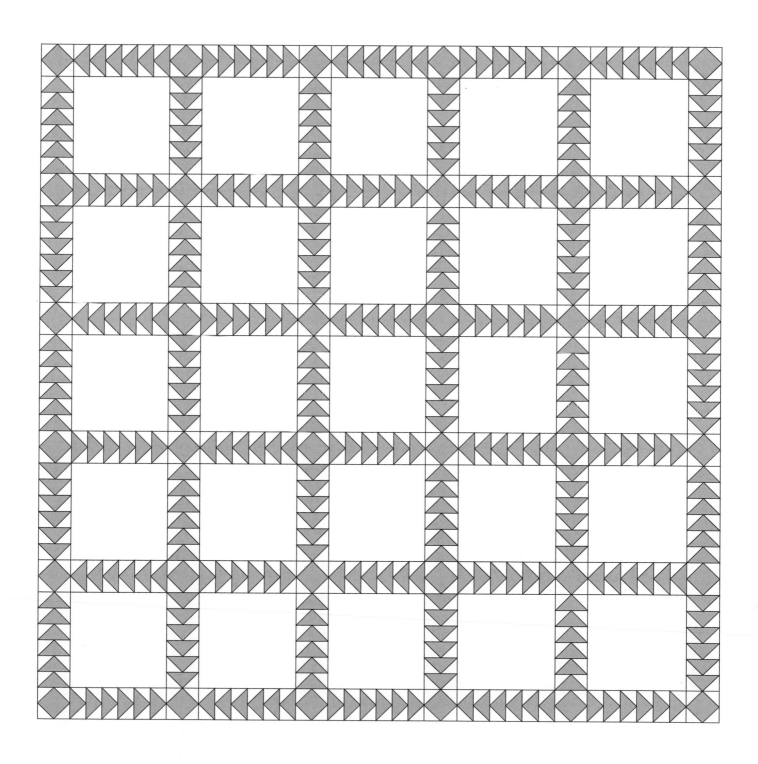

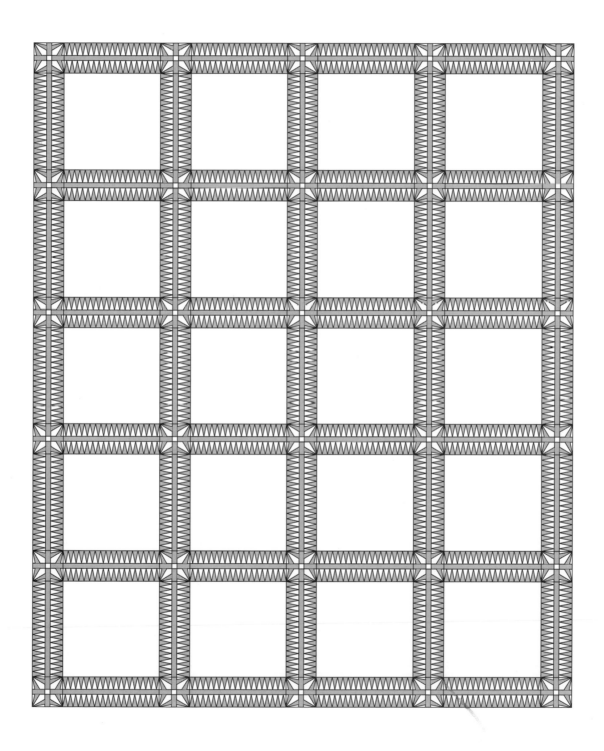

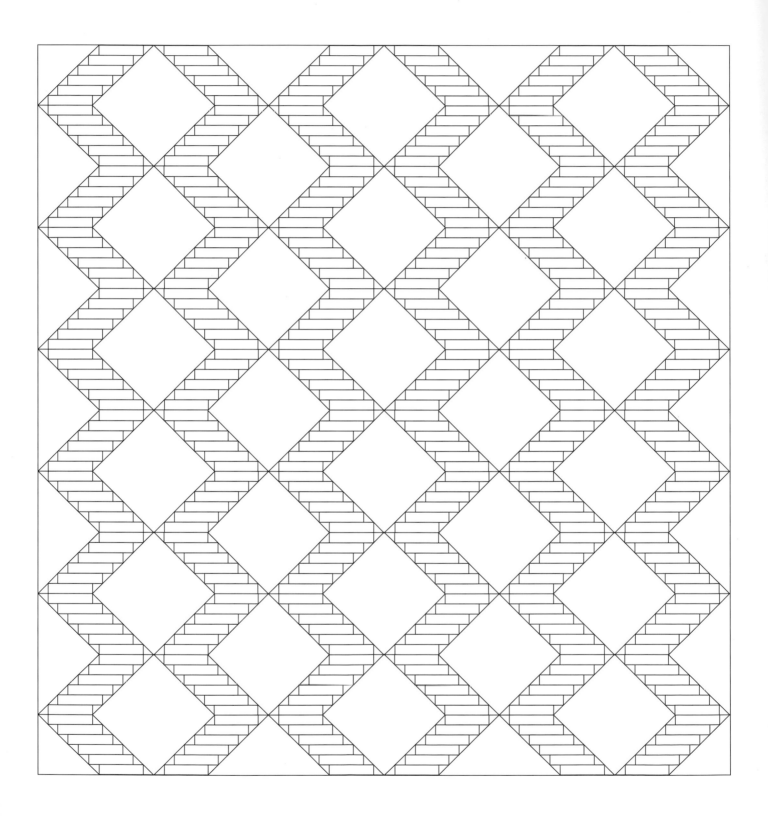

Sets & Sashings for Quilts – Phyllis D. Miller

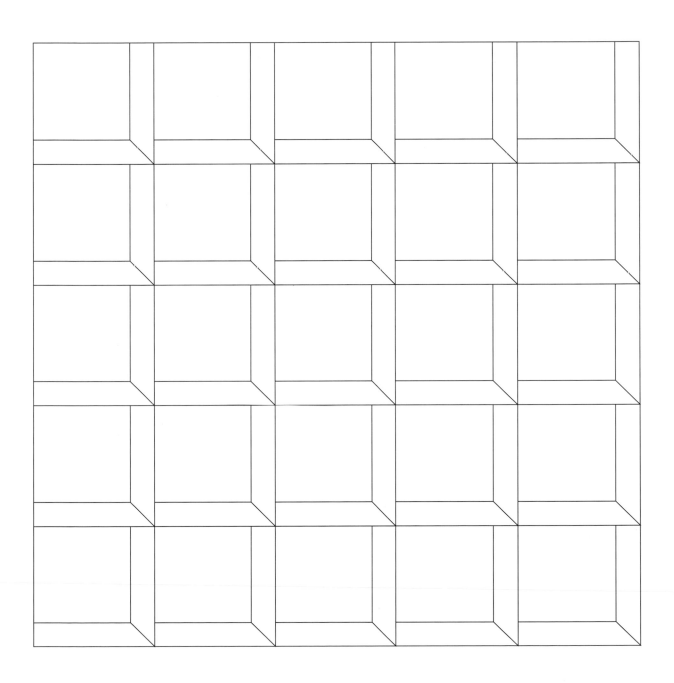

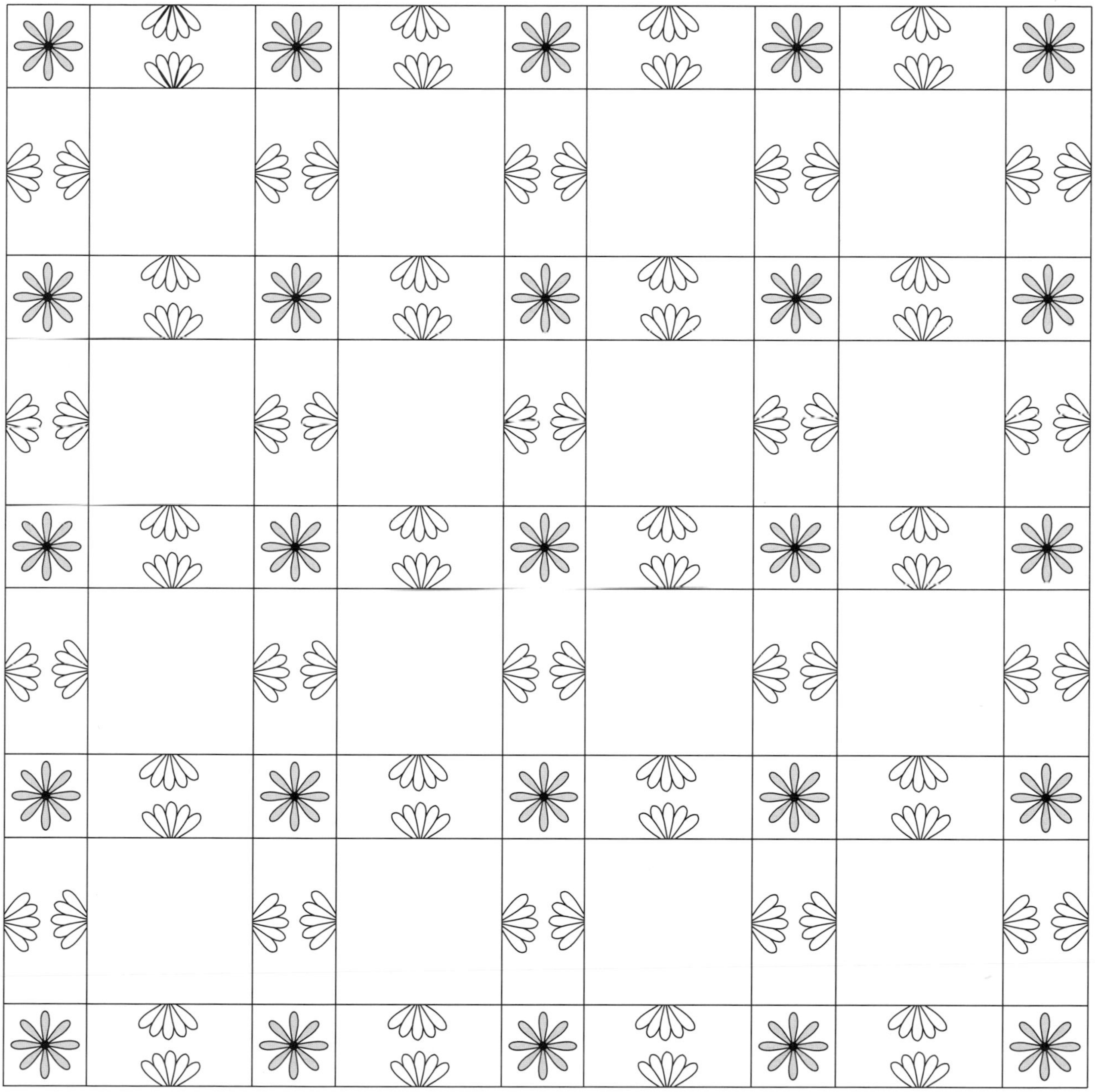

PATTERNS FOR SASHINGS

Patterns for Sawtooth Star Sashing (page 48)

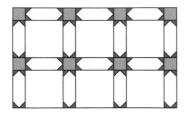

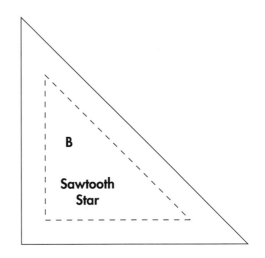

B

Sawtooth Star

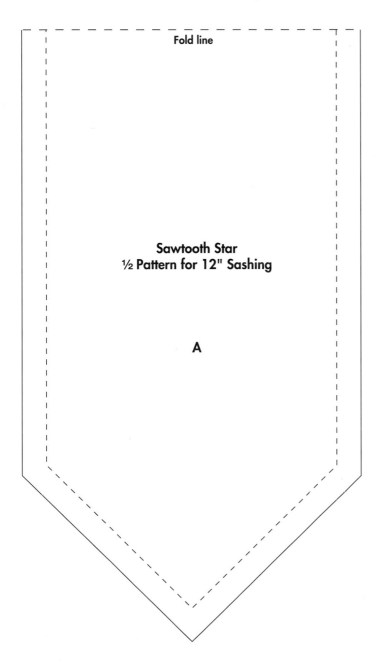

Fold line

Sawtooth Star
½ Pattern for 12" Sashing

A

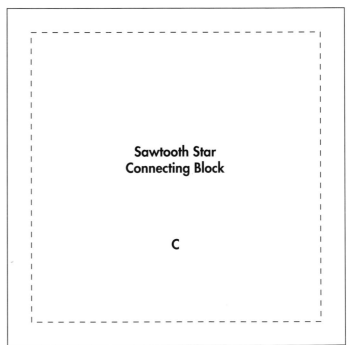

Sawtooth Star
Connecting Block

C

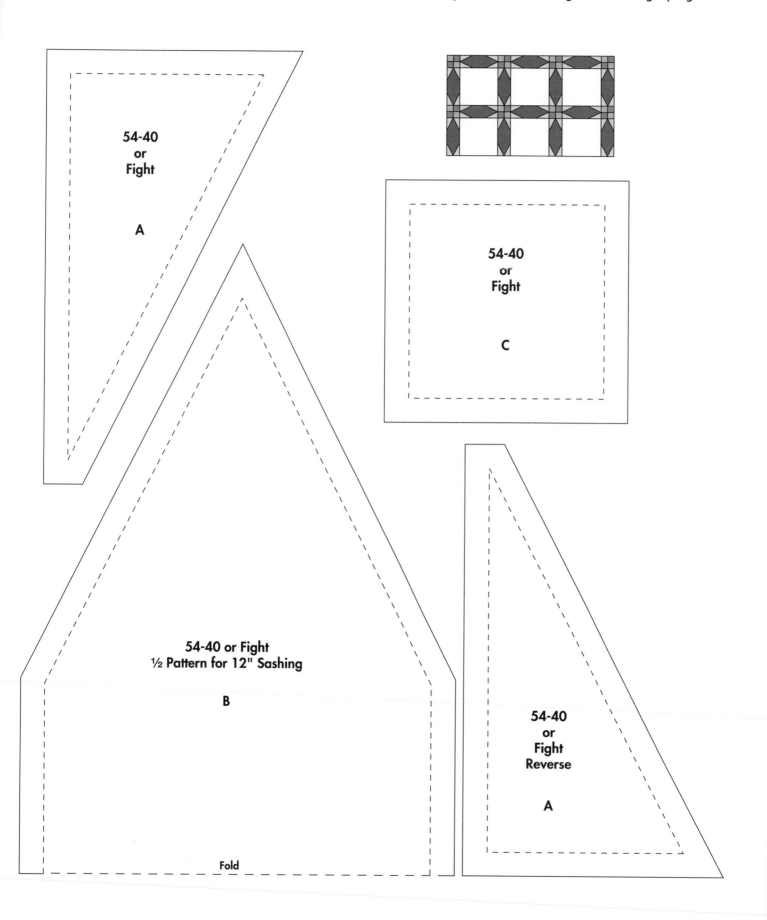

**54-40
or
Fight**

A

**54-40
or
Fight**

C

**54-40 or Fight
½ Pattern for 12" Sashing**

B

**54-40
or
Fight
Reverse**

A

Fold

Patterns for Squares on Point Sashing, top (page 53)
Patterns for Darting Minnow Sashing, bottom (page 55)

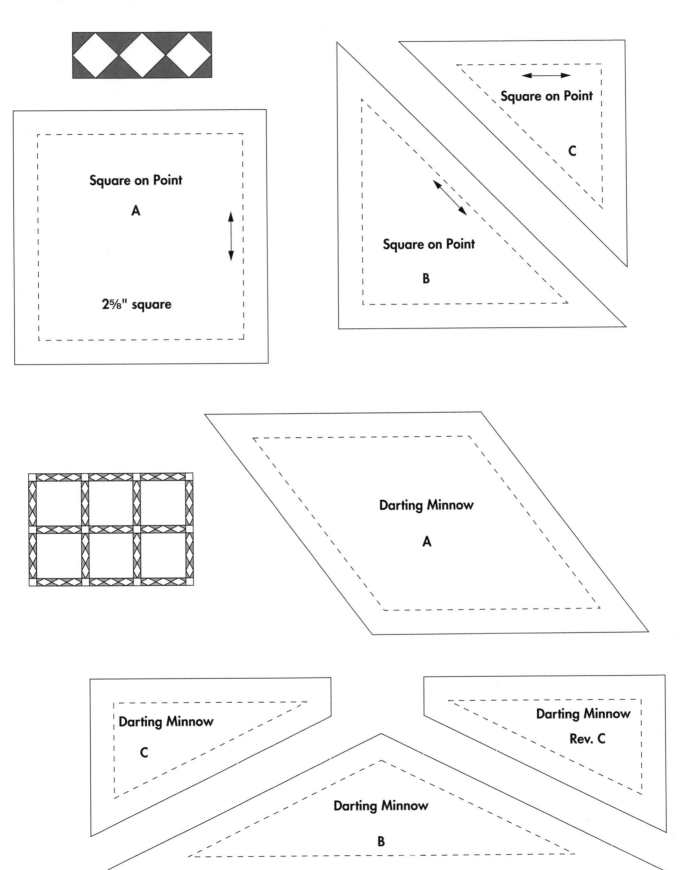

Square on Point

A

2⅝" square

Square on Point

C

Square on Point

B

Darting Minnow

A

Darting Minnow

C

Darting Minnow

Rev. C

Darting Minnow

B

Sets & Sashings for Quilts – Phyllis D. Miller

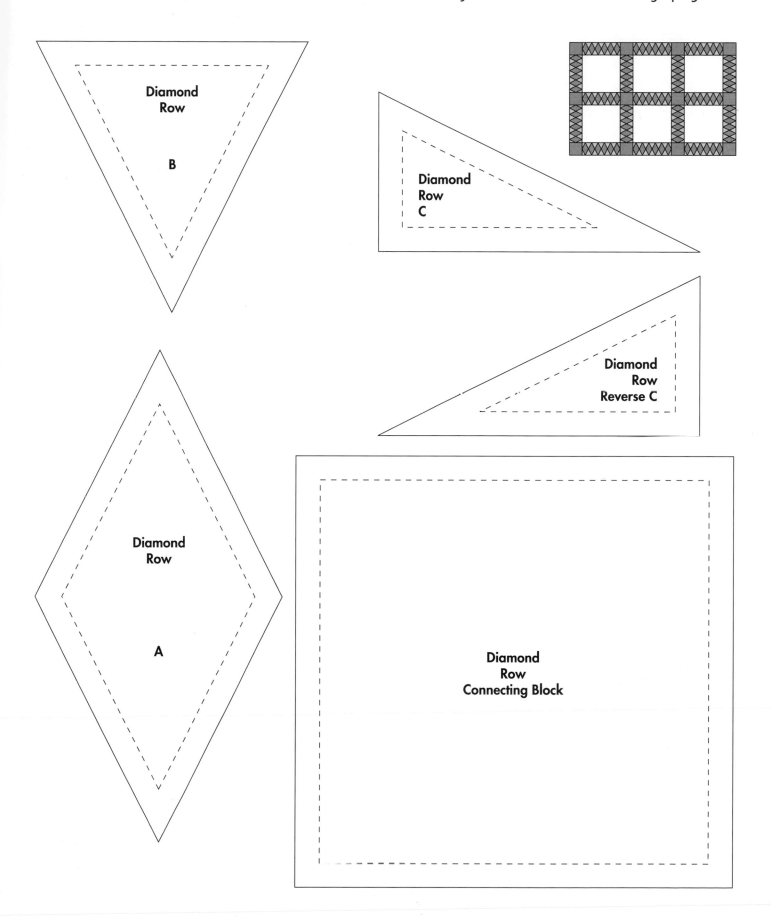

Diamond
Row

B

Diamond
Row
C

Diamond
Row
Reverse C

Diamond
Row

A

Diamond
Row
Connecting Block

Patterns for Braided Sashing (page 58)

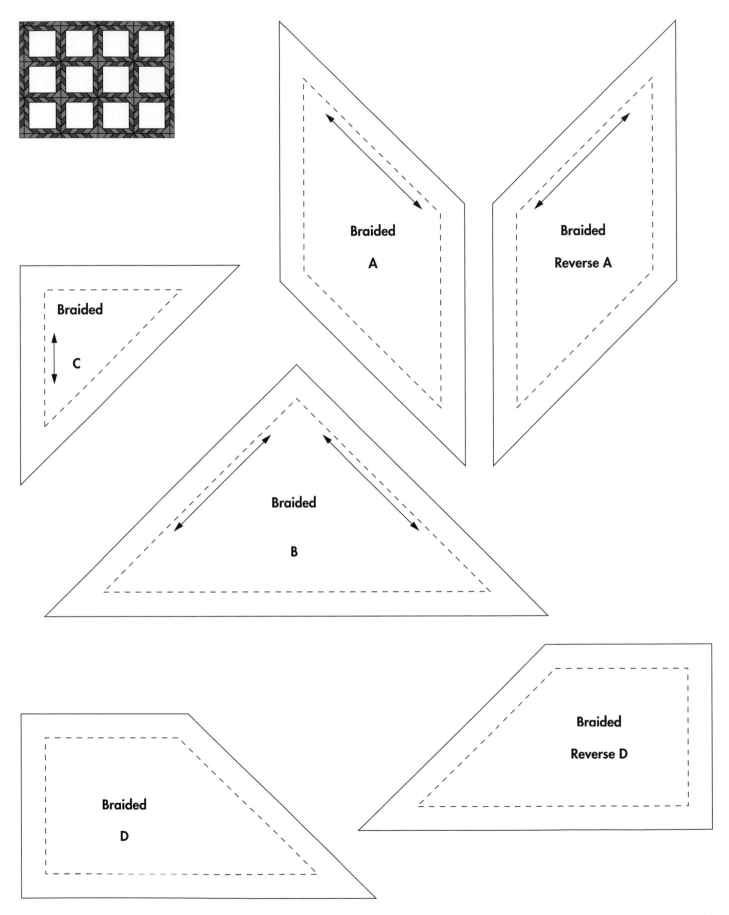

Braided

A

Braided

Reverse A

Braided

C

Braided

B

Braided

Reverse D

Braided

D

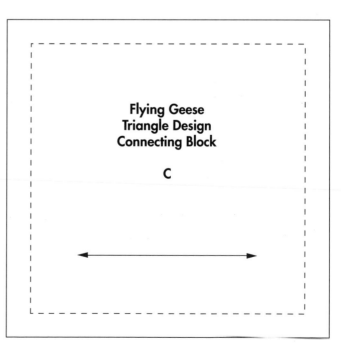

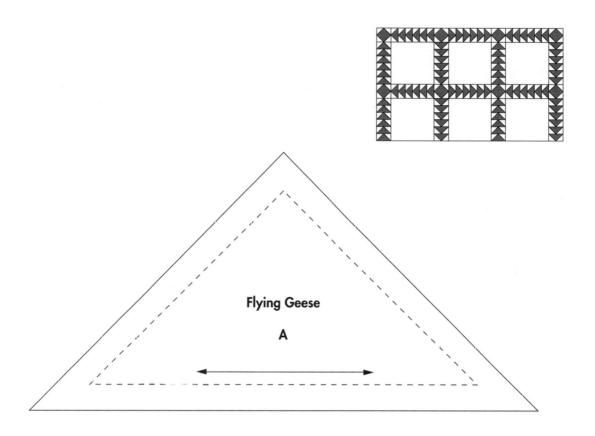

Flying Geese

A

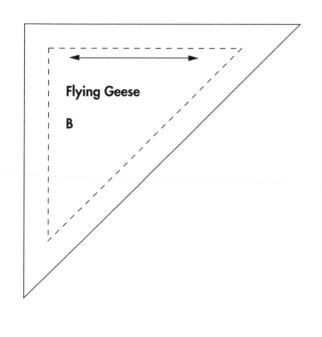

Flying Geese

B

**Flying Geese
Triangle Design
Connecting Block**

C

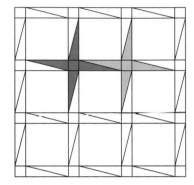

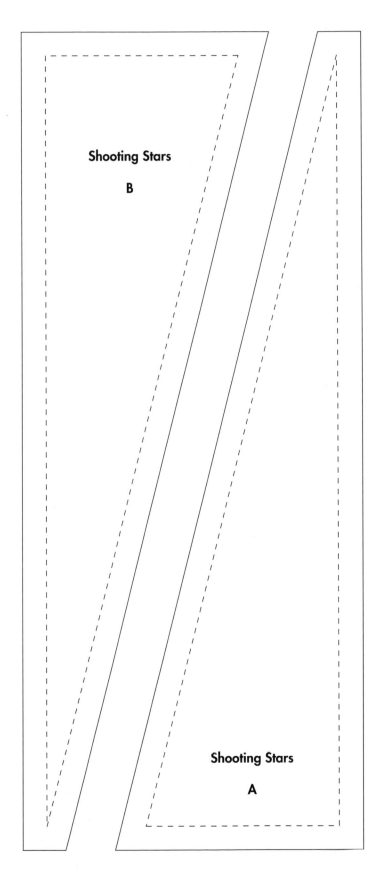

Shooting Stars

B

Shooting Stars

A

**Shooting Stars
Connecting Block**

2½" square

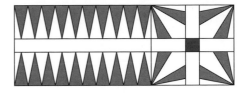

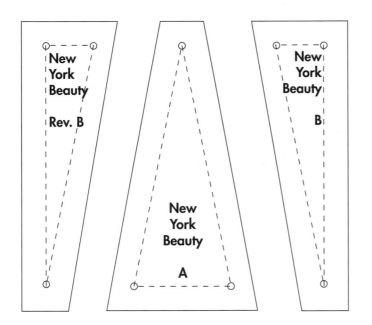

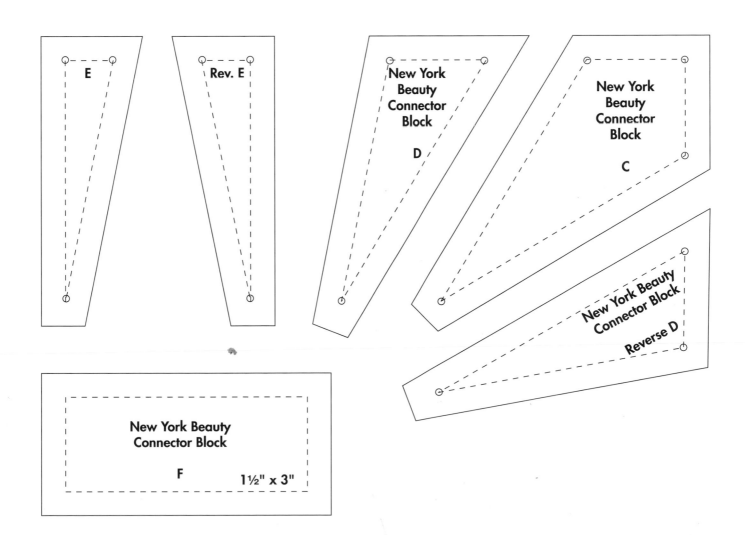

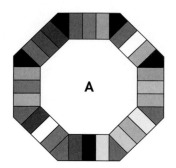

A

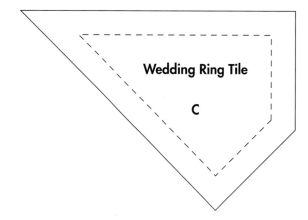

Wedding Ring Tile

B

Wedding Ring Tile

C

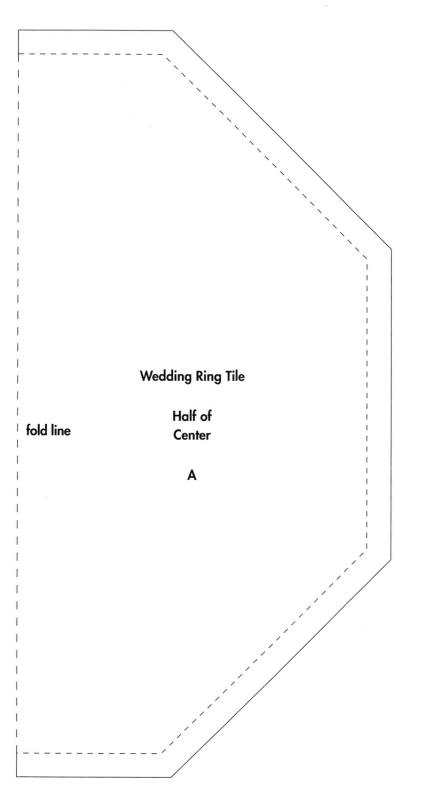

Wedding Ring Tile

Half of
Center

A

fold line

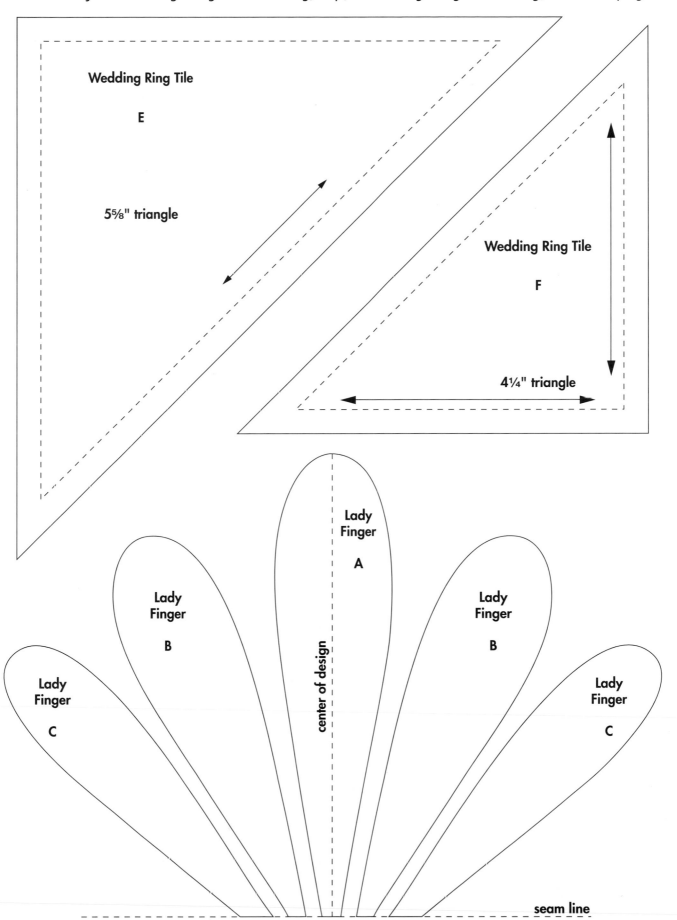

Wedding Ring Tile

E

5⅝" triangle

Wedding Ring Tile

F

4¼" triangle

Lady
Finger

A

Lady
Finger

B

Lady
Finger

C

Lady
Finger

B

Lady
Finger

C

center of design

seam line

Pattern for ¼ of Lady Finger Connector Block, top (page 86)
Patterns for Bridal Stairway, bottom (page 74)

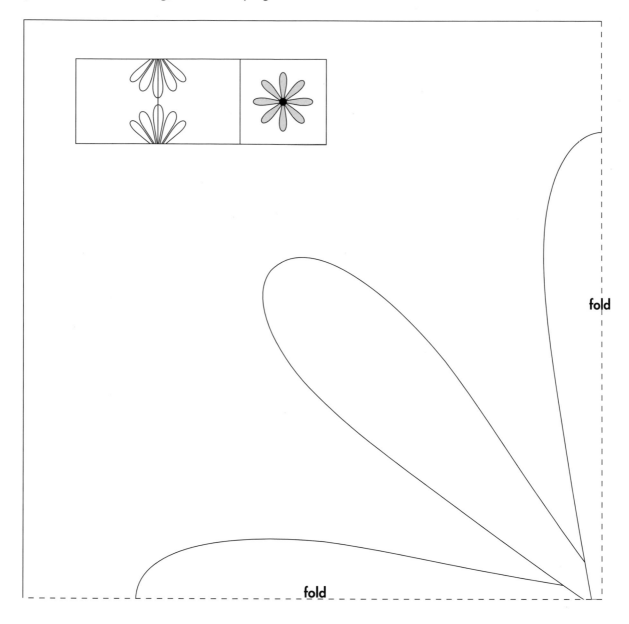

fold

fold

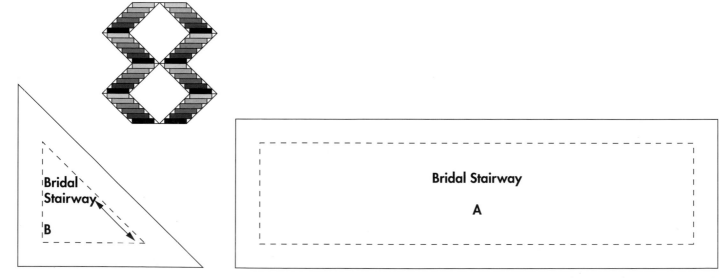

Bridal
Stairway

B

Bridal Stairway

A

Sets & Sashings for Quilts – Phyllis D. Miller

Patterns for Scrolling Vine with Flowers Sashing, left (page 88), and Feather Sashing, right (page 89)

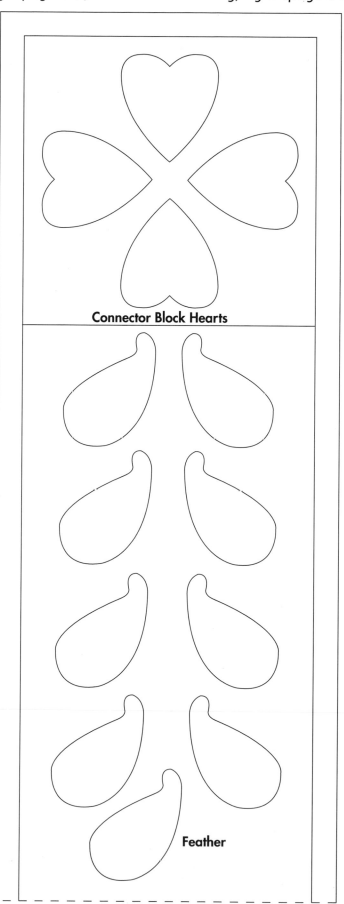

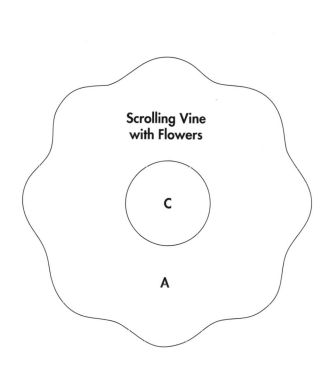

**Scrolling Vine
with Flowers**

C

A

Add seam allowances.

Connector Block Hearts

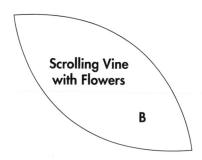

**Scrolling Vine
with Flowers**

B

Feather

fold line for center of sashing strip

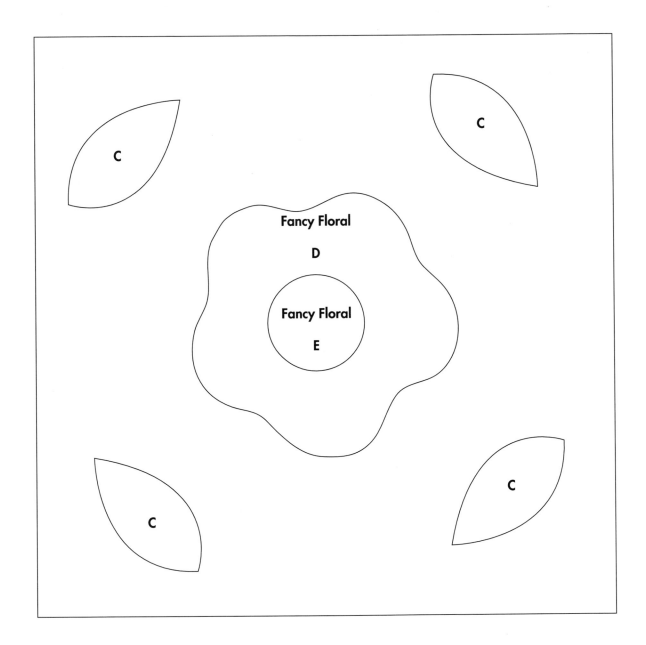

Add seam allowances.

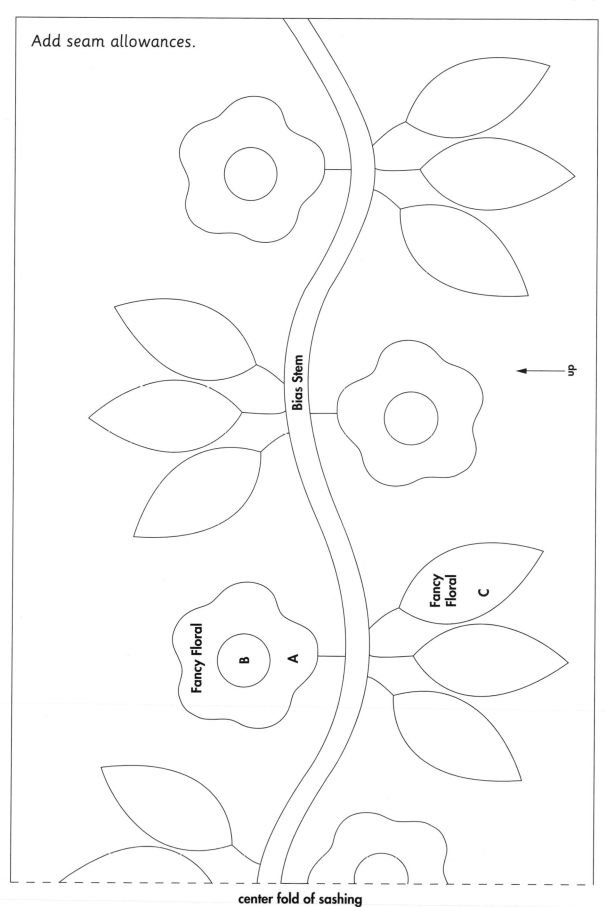

Add seam allowances.

Bias Stem

up

Fancy Floral

B

A

Fancy Floral

C

center fold of sashing

Half of Placement Pattern for Fancy Floral Sashing (page 90)

center fold of sashing

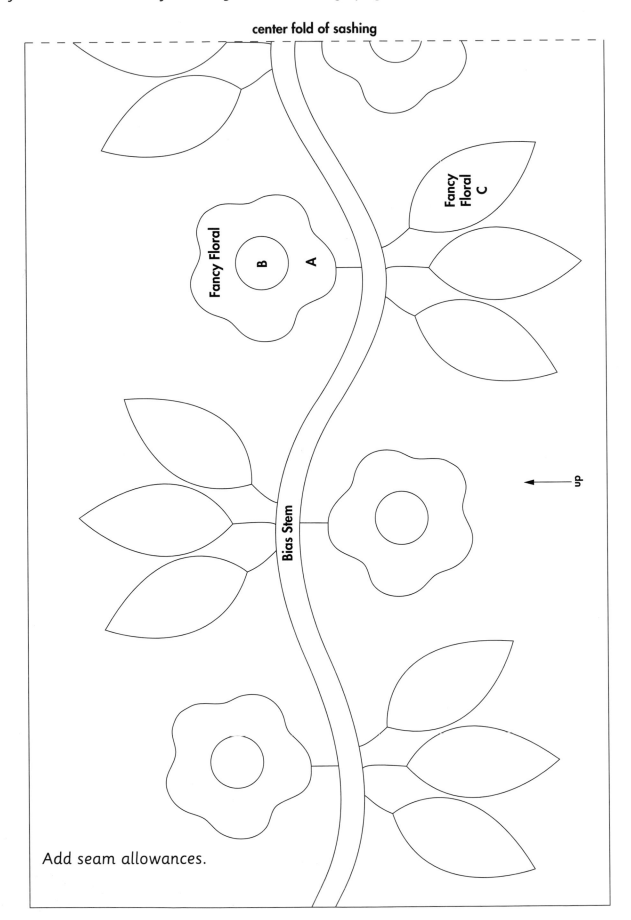

Fancy Floral

B

A

Fancy Floral C

Bias Stem

up

Add seam allowances.

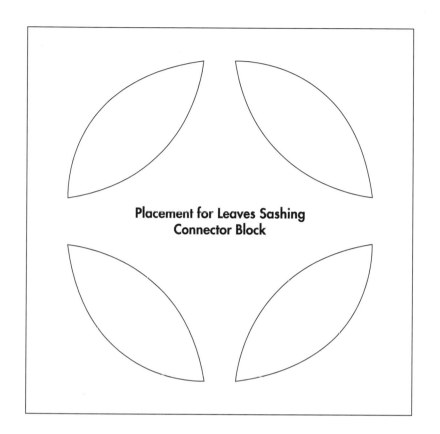

Placement for Leaves Sashing Connector Block

Add seam allowances.

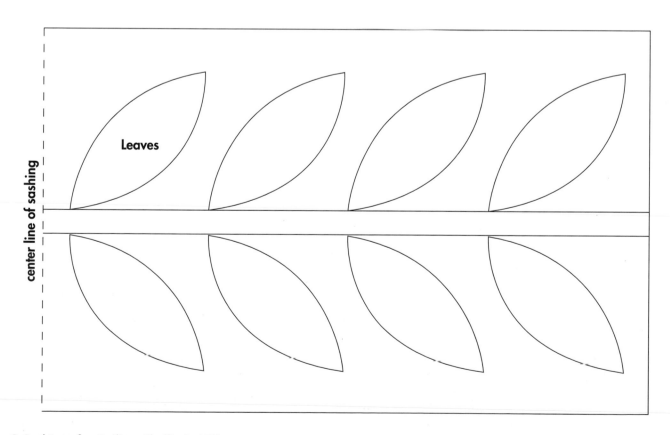

center line of sashing

Leaves

INDEX

BIBLIOGRAPHY

Beyer, Jinny. *Medallion Quilts*. McClean, Virginia: EPM Publications, Inc., 1982.

Brackman, Barbara. *Encyclopedia of Pieced Quilt Patterns*. Paducah, Kentucky: American Quilter's Society, 1993.

Gutcheon, Beth and Jeffrey. *The Quilt Design Workbook*. New York: The Alchemy Press, 1976.

Hall, Carrie A. and Rose Kretsinger. *The Romance of the American Patchwork Quilt*. Mineola, New York: Dover Publications, Inc., 1988.

Hanson, Joan. *Sensational Settings*. Bothell, Washington: That Patchwork Place, Inc., 1993.

Hickey, Mary, Nancy J. Martin, Marsha McCloskey, and Sara Nephew. *Quick and Easy Quiltmaking*. Bothell, Washington: That Patchwork Place, Inc., 1993.

Hassel, Carla J. *Super Quilter II*. Des Moines, Iowa: Wallace-Homestead Book Company, 1982.

Hassel, Carla J. *You Can Be A Super Quilter*. Des Moines, Iowa: Wallace-Homestead Book Company, 1980.

James, Michael. *The Quiltmaker's Handbook*. Englewood Cliffs, New Jersey: Prentice-Hall, Inc., 1978.

Marston, Gwen and Joe Cunningham. *Sets and Borders*. Paducah, Kentucky: American Quilter's Society, 1987.

Miller, Margaret J. *Blockbuster Quilts*. Bothell, Washington: That Patchwork Place, Inc., 1991.

Pellman, Rachel T. *How To Make An Amish Quilt*. Emmaus, Pennsylvania: Rodale Press, 1989.

Ryan, Mildred Graves. *The Complete Encyclopedia of Stitchery*. Garden City, New York: Doubleday & Company, Inc., 1979.

Walker, Michelle. *The Complete Book of Quiltmaking*. London: Ebury Press, 1985.

Williamson, Darra Duffy. *Sensational Scrap Quilts*. Paducah, Kentucky: American Quilter's Society, 1990.

ABOUT THE AUTHOR

Phyllis D. Miller has been making quilts since the summer of 1968 and has made numerous quilts and wallhangings since that time. Her quilts have been exhibited and won awards on the local, state, and national levels.

Phyllis graduated from Berea College, Berea, Kentucky, in 1963 with a B.S. degree in business administration. She is well known in the quilt world as a teacher and for her organizational abilities.

She is an active supporter and member of the Kentucky Heritage Quilt Society which she served as president, editor of the KHQS newsletter, and chair of the Museum and Archives Committee. She was the founder of the Kentucky Heritage Appliqué Society, a KHQS auxiliary group.

Phyllis feels that one of her most rewarding accomplishments was starting Quilter's Day Out in Kentucky so that quilters would have one day each year when they could be together. This was a way to bring a statewide organization to the quilters. This day of celebration was later declared National Quilting Day by the National Quilting Association and is now celebrated around the world.

Her first book, *Encyclopedia of Designs for Quilting*, was published by the American Quilter's Society in 1996.

Phyllis's favorite parts of quilting are designing the quilt and choosing an appropriate design for the quilting. She promotes creative and innovative use of traditional quilt design elements to make every quilt unique. She makes both traditional and contemporary quilts, often combining both ideas in the same piece.

QUILT BOOKS

This is only a small selection of the books available from the American Quilter's Society. AQS books are known worldwide for timely topics, clear writing, beautiful color photos, and accurate illustrations and patterns. These books are available from your local bookseller, quilt shop, or public library.

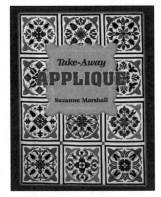

#5012 • $22.95

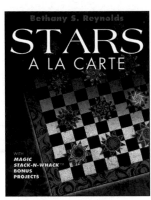

#5589 • $21.95

#5591 • $18.95

#5176 • $24.95

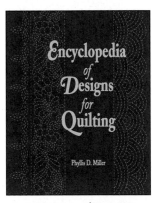

#4814 • $34.95

#5211 • $18.95

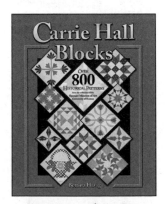

#4957 • $34.95

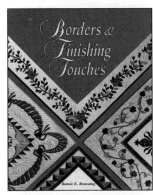

#4898 • $16.95

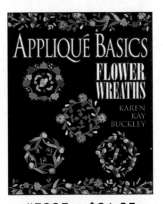

#5335 • $21.95

Look for these books nationally or call
1-800-626-5420.